THE
2% RULE
TO GET
DEBT FREE
FAST

An Innovative Method To Pay Your Loans Off For Good

ALEX & CASSIE MICHAEL
Founders of TheThriftyCouple.com

PAGE STREET
PUBLISHING CO.

PAGE STREET
PUBLISHING CO.

DEDICATION

This book is dedicated to the children that saved us financially: Audrey, Katrina, Nathan, Juliette, Josiah and Jeremiah. You are our why for getting out of debt, our why for establishing ourselves financially and our why for everything we do. We love each of you beyond measure!

CONTENTS

THE HONEYMOON THAT STARTED IT ALL

BY: ALEX

It was the honeymoon of our dreams on the Oregon Coast. Just days before we had one of the most elegant weddings in our little southeast Idaho town—including a grand finale: a full fireworks show. The honeymoon itinerary stated we were to check out of our hotel that morning and make our way to yet another ocean-facing honeymoon suite fully equipped with a Jacuzzi and fireplace. Upon returning to Portland, we were to enjoy an extravagant dinner at the fanciest restaurant I could book at a price easily over $100 for the meal and then fly home the next day. Yes, it was going to be the perfect end to the perfect honeymoon.

I was checking out of the hotel when the voice of the front desk clerk startled me: "Mr. Michael, your card was declined. Do you have another?"

I became paralyzed as my mind raced from one thought to another. I didn't have another card. Well, I had another card, but it was the debit card associated with my checking account that I had drained making preparations for our wedding. I knew for a fact there wasn't enough balance to check out of a luxurious, beachside hotel; at this point, a simple donut and coffee could have sent that account into the negative.

I was completely shocked by this situation.

We had been planning this wedding for over a year. In fact, our lives had been consumed by it, as we knew the wedding my bride wanted was outside all our budgets. Cassie's parents acknowledged they could pay a certain amount, but it wouldn't cover many of the extras that she wanted at that time. So, what was I supposed to do? I promised to help pay for the wedding to ensure that Cassie received the wedding she had been dreaming of all her life; those extras resulted in a loan to finance that wedding of our dreams.

Those little things drained our budget. My bank account was at zero, and I couldn't check out of the hotel. Which led me to a local branch of our bank in that small coastal town to get a loan.

I sat down with the loan officer and filled out a quick form. The loan officer complimented me on my credit score. I mention that here because it would be one of the last times that I would hear that. Of course my credit score was good. At the time, I only had three student loans that I was paying off and the loan for our wedding.

I had mentioned to the loan officer that we were on our honeymoon and ran into a bit of an issue with our hotel. What I hadn't communicated to her was the terror surging through my body throughout this whole process. What would happen if we weren't approved? It seemed like time had stopped. I watched the clock—it hadn't stopped—but the seconds ticked by so slowly.

The loan officer came back to her desk. I still remember watching her face. She smiled, but not in a way that guaranteed me the answer I wanted to hear. Maybe she was just trying to be nice before she told me that she could see the financial risk we would become, that the bank could tell by my non-verbal communication that we would one day amass over one hundred thousand dollars of consumer debt, and they didn't want anything to do with us.

She must have seen my face because she immediately assured me that the loan was approved and that the news was even better than expected. The credit line was for way more than I had asked, even more than I had wanted. Instead of a couple thousand dollars, we were approved for $7,500.

At that point, I didn't really process the total amount. I started to feel relief and was excited to go back to the hotel and share with my love that we could check out. Everything was going to be all right.

I signed my life away. Not once did I consider how much this loan would cost us, both in interest and in the financial despair that was to come.

I honestly can't remember many details from the rest of our honeymoon, but I can promise it was lavish. We did stay at that honeymoon suite the next night. We did make it back to Portland for dinner at that expensive, fancy restaurant. While we were eating that last night in Oregon, our honeymoon ended just the way it had started—with fireworks right next to the restaurant. You would think this might have been one of the most romantic events up to that point in our young marriage, but strangely enough, the magic you would expect was missing.

I'm not sure to this day what it was, but I know what it should have been: an empty nagging that the path we were headed down would land us in despair and misery long before it would get better.

Chapter 1

Why You Need This Book

By: Alex

In the morning, you wake up late for work because you were up so late the night before. You click the snooze button a few extra times to get the sleep you so desperately need, yet you still wake up groggy, relying on coffee, chocolate and then soda throughout the day to get that extra energy you're depending on.

Already late, you notice you didn't have time the night before to set the coffee maker to go off. Instead, you wind up stopping by the coffee shop on the way to work (more money spent out of pocket) and pick up a bagel while you're at it (more empty carbs) because you just didn't have time to make yourself a healthier breakfast. The barista knows your name, as this isn't the first time you slept through your alarm or that you missed making your coffee. Sure, the experts share that breakfast is the most important meal of the day; one day you hope to actually accomplish that.

As your morning grinds on, your boss reminds you that the report she asked for a few weeks ago is due by end of the day. You mutter a few words under your breath and stammer that it will get done like it always does. The only problem is the way it always does is in a rush and without the kind of quality you would expect from someone if they were working for you.

Nearing lunch, your co-workers start planning which restaurant they hope to visit today. You quietly calculate the total cost of your lunches out this month and realize you could have made a significant dent in your credit card balance this month had you brought your own lunch. Oh well, what's another day? Maybe you can start making a lunch to bring to work . . . next week.

After being gone for a lunch that consisted of too much rich food and a bit longer than you expected, you realize that report really needs to get done. You start working on it and end up leaving the office an hour later than you were hoping and turning in a less than perfect report.

Upon leaving the office, you realize your family is going to be famished by the time you get home. There's no way you can expect them to wait for you to plan and cook a healthy meal by the time you walk in the door. You realize it's Tuesday, meaning you can stop at a local drive-in and buy the whole family tacos, thankful that some genius came up with that amazing Taco Tuesday.

On the last minutes of the drive, you realize you just ate out for all three meals of the day. Let's face it, it's expensive and not the healthiest way to live, but what other way is there?

You get home to find the house a bit disorganized, the kitchen needing a bit of tidying, and then your spouse reminds you that guests are coming over in less than 30 minutes. You all quickly scarf down your meal of tacos and frantically work to clean and prepare for your guests to come over.

After a full night of company and helping your kids with their homework, you drag yourself to your bedroom to find your bed in the same mess you left it in that morning. You think about those experts again and remember that one of them might have stated how much better it was to air your bedding out anyway, so you claim success although your mind might be in a bit of disarray from the disorganization and mess of the room.

Finally, you crawl into bed and either stream your favorite sitcoms that you missed from the day before or watch the late show, hoping a few jokes might calm you down.

As you finally drift off to sleep, you realize that you're about an hour past your ideal bedtime. Those experts keep recommending you set a bedtime and stick with it; maybe one day you'll actually do it. Just before the sweet release into sleep, you're jarred awake when you realize you forgot to set the coffee maker, and you forgot to get the meat out of the freezer for the next day's dinner.

Maybe tomorrow will be different.

Does this day sound familiar to you at all? It sure does to us because in our years of debt accumulation and attempting to pay off our debt we were letting life fly.

No one really plans to get into debt, financial woes or financial struggles. For so many, you live life and before you know it, you are in a lot of debt, and you aren't completely sure how you got there, what you have to show for it or how this happened.

You've picked up this book for whatever reason. Maybe you are in a little bit of debt and need some tips and encouragement to become debt free. But maybe you are deep in debt and feeling completely lost, hopeless and at the end of your financial rope.

We were that couple at the end of our financial rope. We were that couple that had sunk so low on the debt-boat. We were hopeless. We could see no way out. We were stuck. We had over $108,000 of consumer debt.

As you read this book, you will read excerpts from our financial story: one that is part soap opera and part primetime drama and yes, very often, you may shake your head in disbelief at our stupidity.

So, Why Should You Listen To Us?

Because we've been there! And we were able to climb our way out. We paid off over $108,000 of debt in a short amount of time.

Our plan not only shares how to get out of debt step-by-step, but also how to stay out. We promote a lifestyle of financial wisdom and debt freedom via slow, gradual change while encouraging a sustainable lifestyle the whole journey. We show you how to take the intentional steps you need to take back control of your lives.

Other plans require that you change your lifestyle overnight, dropping everything and slashing your budgets by 80 percent and eating rice and beans until the end. We had dozens of false starts. We'd attempt to follow those plans and wake up that super-frugal, debt-slashing couple each day. But the second we flubbed up, we felt like failures, hopeless again. It seemed that nearly weekly we'd tell each other we'd failed again because we went over budget, or we'd gone out to eat when our new budget didn't allow, or we'd bought new shoes when we shouldn't have. We'd say, "We will start again on Monday," only to repeat the same sentence a few days later. It was very frustrating. We kept setting ourselves up for failure. We couldn't meet the demands of the debt payoff plans. It was a crash diet that was not sustainable.

How could we get out of debt if we could hardly even get out of the gate? Then, if we successfully made all the sacrifices, how would we stay out of debt and not keep jumping back into it? It just didn't work for us.

How Did We Get Here?

Many of our debts were obviously foolish. We look back today and realize that much of our debt was obtained by eating out or traveling—because we wanted to do it all when we were young. Funny thing, those restaurants and most of the trips are all a blur now. The pain, the turmoil and hardships we experienced from going into that much debt stick with us even today.

But as you will see, it wasn't just mindless spending that added up to that total amount of debt. It was debt accrued from car loans, one-of-a-kind deals and keeping-up-appearances purchases.

For example, who hasn't had someone knock on your door and share with you how much cleaner your home would be if you purchased their vacuum, one that will be the last vacuum you'll ever need to buy? Well, not only did they sell us the vacuum, which we could not pay cash for, but it came with a hefty 22.97% APR (annual percentage rate) which made the amount we paid significantly more than the original price by a lot. We also bought a water softener the same way at a lower 17.99% APR. The rate was lower than that of the vacuum, but still so high we shudder at the amount we really paid.

We've since learned that although products might be of the highest quality, is it really worth the debt you might incur to purchase them? The words, "This will be the last product of this type you'll ever need" are never true...

There were also other charges that seemed to be more justifiable, like buying furniture to fill a newly bought house or buying jewelry as special gifts for my wife to make her feel more special and know how I really felt for Valentine's Day.

First, it was the furniture. After buying our first home, we had so much empty space after moving from our small apartment. So we did what we thought everyone did: go shopping at the furniture store and maximize the amazing deals they were offering.

We found the couch, the loveseat, coffee and sofa tables and the kitchen dining set that we just had to have. The salesman was a huge help taking care of us throughout the whole process, even asking us how we were planning to pay for the items. This was still early in our process of accumulating debt, so a little lump crept up in my throat until he confirmed that we could just easily apply for their store credit account and should be out of there in no time.

It was so easy! Just fill out a form and then wait 15 to 20 minutes for them to come back with their answer. But, here's the rub: that furniture we purchased had a nice 21.00% APR that came along with it. We had so many preconceived notions going into home buying that we wish we hadn't developed, like needing to furnish an empty house so we could entertain guests. Much of that furniture has long ago been replaced due to age, but the memories of friends that visited with us, who couldn't have cared less whether we had an expensive, debt-ridden table or a card table we bought at a discount store, remain. If only we had known what was important and what would last.

Then something else started to happen—we started finding it harder and harder to keep up with payments and keep the bill collectors at bay.

Then help came, right into our mailbox!

Have you ever received those bulk mailings offering the recipient a loan for up to a few thousand dollars, and all you had to do was cash the check? Maybe it was a guaranteed loan offer and all you needed to do was to come into their office to set it up? If you wonder who actually would acquire one of those loans with astounding interest rates, well now you know.

We knew we were having problems making our payments on our loans and needed money fast. Of course, I probably didn't need to tell you that we were somehow able to still justify our lifestyle of eating extravagantly and making our small weekend trips.

Yes, we were so desperate that we got one of those loans. As I write this, I'm still aghast at the 36.00% APR just to borrow $1,000. The top of the letter reads, "Simple. Convenient.

Timely. Useful." Odd that it doesn't include the words costly and selling your soul, but these loans seemed like such a gift at the time when we got them. They didn't require a credit check and that particular one had the instructions, "Just endorse the attached loan check and deposit it in your bank account" in bold at the top of the letter. I mean, not only did I not have to have my credit checked, but I also didn't have to face the embarrassment of meeting a loan agent face to face with the probability of walking out red faced and empty-handed.

You see, these companies prey on those that are grabbing at straws financially. They are waiting right there with the promise you can use the money any way you want. Seriously, this loan offer letter promises it can be used for anything including a special purchase, paying off credit card bills, fixing up the car or house or even enjoying a weekend getaway.

This is where it gets scary. Getting these loans was easy. Paying them back was nearly impossible.

Loan after loan, we continued down the rabbit hole. It had to come to an end, and finally it did. At least, until we were really needing money with nowhere else to turn.

Those were the days I had to swallow my pride even more, face my shame head on and walk into my first Pay Day loan office. If I thought 36.00% APR was bad, just wait. It got worse, MUCH worse.

That's why after all the tears and stress we came up with a new, permanent, achievable method to ditch the debt for good! And friends, this is where our 2% Rule was born! If we were a couple that could so foolishly dive so deep into debt, and the 2% Rule worked to help us get out of debt, then anyone can achieve debt freedom.

No matter where you have been, we encourage you to keep reading and get excited that it really is possible to pay off your debt and meet your financial goals. Let's dive right into the heart of the plan to show you just how easy it is to get started. Before you know it, you just might be celebrating your new debt-free status. Know that we'll be celebrating right along with you.

Read on to learn the steps necessary to become debt free using our 2% Rule.

Chapter 2

What Is The 2% Rule?

By: Alex

We call this our 2% Rule because we only make changes in 2 percent intervals. Unlike the crash-diet-80-percent-budget-slashing that other debt programs require, we only ask that you apply 2 percent changes. Our gradual approach consists of a small decrease each month in expenses and a small increase in income.

First we will share the heart of our 2% Rule and then break down some of the principles. Don't worry if you have questions. Remember, this whole book is meant to teach you this approach, so those questions you have now will be answered by the time you read the last page.

At the heart of the 2% Rule is the idea of gradual change. We knew that it took us years to rack up the amount of debt we were in when we started our journey. We knew that it took years for us to establish our patterns for living that were internalized deep within us. We learned during our early years of debt reduction that changing those patterns wasn't something we could do overnight. It would take time to change those habits, and it would take time to dig ourselves out of the mess that it took years for us to get into.

The 2% Rule

The 2% Rule: Track your monthly expenses and earnings. Use this actual information for the following month to decrease spending by 2 percent and increase income by 2 percent.

It almost sounds too basic, doesn't it? The reality of this plan is that it uses some basic common sense. It doesn't need to be complicated, and it factors in where you are now and helps you apply small, gradual change to get you where you want to be.

Implementing The 2% Rule

Here are the six steps you will follow to implement the 2% Rule:

1. Track your expenses and earnings for a month

2. Create your baseline budget based on the results from Step 1

3. Decrease spending the following month by 2 percent

4. Increase income the following month by 2 percent

5. Apply the "found money" from steps 3 and 4 towards your financial goals

6. Each month repeat steps 3 through 5

Let's break each step down and discuss both the hows and the whys.

Step 1. Track your expenses and earnings

Where this plan differs from most is that we want you to see where you are today. The goal is not to ask you to consider and plan on paper the minimum crash diet budget you think your family can follow. The goal is not to have you sit as a family and pore through hours of paperwork trying to figure out all the expenses you plan to cut from the very start to trim your budget down to almost nothing.

No, your first step is simply to track this month's expenses. Don't worry, this is not a long, arduous research project but instead can be done in one of two simple ways.

The first method is to simply track your normal spending over the course of a month. We encourage you to group your expenses into categories, as it will make it easier to find places to cut in future months by determining where most of your money is going.

You can use the following quick list of sample categories to start. Obviously, this is just a list of high-level categories that will fit many families; your family may wish to add other categories specific to you and leave off others that are not relevant:

Living Expenses

- Groceries
- Gasoline
- Clothing
- Entertainment
- Eating Out
- Home Improvement
- Christmas and Other Holidays
- Travel
- Miscellaneous Shopping (e.g., crafts, school supplies)

Bills

- Auto
- Insurance
- Utilities
- Cell Phones
- Internet
- Cable
- Services/Fees

The second method is relevant to those of you that have been tracking your spending habits either by using an online tool or other tracking method. Many of you might be using a credit card for most of your expenses. If you are, I encourage you to check your credit card account and see if they offer you a breakdown of the types of expenses you are making each and every month.

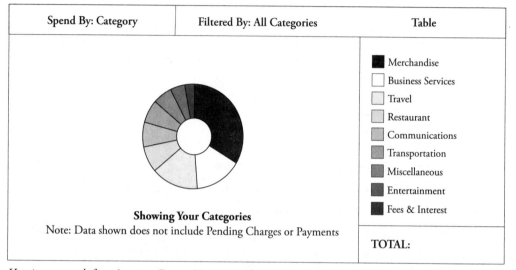

Spend By: Category	Filtered By: All Categories	Table
		■ Merchandise
		□ Business Services
		☐ Travel
		▨ Restaurant
		▨ Communications
		▨ Transportation
		▨ Miscellaneous
		▨ Entertainment
		■ Fees & Interest
Showing Your Categories Note: Data shown does not include Pending Charges or Payments		**TOTAL:**

Here is an example from American Express. You can see above just how easily they break down the charges based on stores and categorize your spending for you. This isn't an encouragement to use an American Express credit card, but rather just to give you a guide of what you might expect to see on your own credit card website.

What's great is if you use some type of non-cash payment method (credit card, debit card or even check) for a majority of purchases, you now have all those expenses painlessly tracked in a single location and already categorized. You can review and change categories for certain purchases, and even better, split some transactions into multiple categories without breaking a sweat.

Petco	Pet Food & Supply	-$1.22
Ayara Thai Cuisine	Restaurants	-$35.52
Walgreens	Pharmacy	-$10.00
Kohl's	Clothing	-$21.28
CVS	Pharmacy	-$7.26
Dollar Tree	Shopping	-$3.17
Trader Joe's	Groceries	-$58.18

If your credit card company doesn't provide you that type of access (or for those of you who use a debit card), you can use a free on-line service or an app from someone such as Mint.com and sync your credit cards and transactions from your checking account. This is set up to track ALL your expenses from both your bank account and your credit cards in order to manage your budget and spending in one place.

You are also going to track your income from the month, which is usually a little easier than tracking expenses! You need to know your baseline income so you will know your starting place for setting your goal of bringing in an additional 2% income. Make sure you track the income for you and your spouse in this process.

No matter what method you use to track your expenses and income, there are only two ground rules to follow. Make sure you understand these so you track the right expenses for the right amount of time.

Only track your normal expenses during this time. Emergency expenses like car repairs or emergency room visits fit into a special category.

Only track your normal income during this time. Do not include those welcome bursts of income like a nice tax refund.

Try to keep it as simple as possible. Doing otherwise will just set you up to fail.

Step 2. Establish your baseline budget

All you need to do is look at the totals from the last month you tracked and set that as your baseline budget. Really, that's it. The goal of this step is to keep it simple. No need to crunch numbers, compute statistical calculations and jump through hoops to get this budget set up.

So let's look at an example. Pretend that the last month your expenses totaled $3000 and your income was $3000. First, we would applaud you for not spending more than you earned. Many do, which is why they go into so much debt. Trust us, we know. This step allows you to set these baseline numbers needed for the next step.

	Baseline	**Month: February**		**Month: March**	
	Actuals	Planned	Actuals	Planned	Actuals
Total Income	$3,000.00				
Total Expenses	$3,000.00				
Income minus Expenses	$0				

Are you ready? Here comes the fun part!

Step 3. Decrease spending the following month by 2 percent

Set your next month's budget by simply decreasing the current month's by 2 percent. That's your budget for the new month.

So back to our example:

	Baseline	Month: February		Month: March	
	Actuals	Planned	Actuals	Planned	Actuals
Total Income	$3,000.00				
Total Expenses	$3,000.00	$2,940.00			
Income minus Expenses	$0				

Notice we have updated the planned expenses for the next month. All we did was subtract 2 percent from the baseline, and that amount became the new goal for the next month.

Let's break it down so we can be very clear:

- Baseline: $3,000

- Decrease by 2%: $3,000 × 0.02 = $60 (the amount to decrease by)

- New Month: $3,000 − $60 = $2,940

Step 4. Increase your income the following month by 2 percent

You are also going to set a goal of increasing your income for the next month.

	Baseline	Month: February		Month: March	
	Actuals	Planned	Actuals	Planned	Actuals
Total Income	$3,000.00	$3,060.00			
Total Expenses	$3,000.00	$2,940.00			
Income minus Expenses	$0	$120.00			

First, let's break it down so you can clearly see what we've done:

- Baseline Income: $3,000

- Increase by 2%: $3,000 × 0.02 = $60 (the amount to increase by)

- New Month: $3,000 + $60 = $3,060

Step 5. Apply the money from steps 3 and 4 to your financial goals

Do you see the planned remaining amount just after one month? Yes, we're talking about an additional planned $120 available just after one month that you can add to your financial goals. Can you see just how quickly this gradual change can start making an impact in your family's finances?

Step 6. Each month repeat steps 3 through 5

Every month you will track your actual expenses and income, then devise a budget for the following month.

How the 2% Rule Works in Practice

	Baseline	Month: February		Month: March	
	Actuals	Planned	Actuals	Planned	Actuals
Total Income	$3,000.00	$3,060.00	$3,113.00		
Total Expenses	$3,000.00	$2,940.00	$2,968.57		
Income minus Expenses	$0	$120.00	$144.43		

Let's look a bit more closely at how this sample month turned out for this family. First, let's take a look at the expenses. See how the goal for the month of February was $2,940.00 but the actual turned out to be $2,968.57? Should this family give up their plan and walk away to declare failure? No way! They actually did decrease their budget, even if it was not as much as they originally wanted.

In fact, they could have increased their spending over the baseline budget. We know about that, because it has happened to us. The following month we just kept moving forward with the small, gradual goal to spend 2 percent less than the actual results from that month. There wasn't any falling off the wagon or feeling of failure. We just had to pull ourselves together, set the next gradual decrease from that prior month's actual spending, and move forward with our new goal.

Now, let's review the income. This is where it can get quickly exciting! The goal was to increase by just $60, but this family was able to do more, which is common. Especially at first, many families are able to increase over and above that 2 percent goal.

What did all this do for their financial goals? Whereas they were hoping to see an additional $120 to apply to their debt, instead they were able to apply $144.43. Do you see just how awesome that turned out after just one month?

The Next Step

Now that we take the current month's actual numbers and set the planned amounts for the new month:

	Baseline	Month: February		Month: March	
	Actuals	Planned	Actuals	Planned	Actuals
Total Income	$3,000.00	$3,060.00	$3,113.00	$3,175.26	
Total Expenses	$3,000.00	$2,940.00	$2,968.57	$2,909.20	
Income minus Expenses	$0	$120.00	$144.43	$266.06	

Using the information shared above you can see how this was calculated, but we don't want you to miss this final point. The budget and income goals for the following month are 2 percent less and 2 percent more, respectively, than the actual numbers from the month before.

This is where the plan gets exciting and stays real for your family. You may not meet your goals each and every month. That's OK. The next month, your goal is to simply be 2 percent better than you were last month.

This is the step that keeps you from feeling like you're falling behind each month. Each month starts new and fresh without thinking you'll have to really tighten your belt this month to make up for lost progress.

This plan was designed to help you use gradual progress—those baby steps—to meet your financial goals. This final step is the one that really completes the whole cycle and keeps you from stopping.

Wrapping It Up

So, in the end, this is the heart of our plan. We hope you see how slow, gradual change can quickly result in a huge impact in your finances. Obviously, there's a lot to work out in these next few chapters. The goal here was simply to demonstrate our plan. Remember, this wasn't just our theoretical plan we developed in a vacuum. This was the actual plan we used to pay off over $90,000 in just over three years and that we still use today to achieve all our financial goals.

But there is actually more to our plan, much more. If you follow the 2% Rule to get out of debt, that's great. But what we want to show you is a whole financial package for building your financial security.

Here is a summary of the steps. As you work your way through the book, you will discover the importance of each step and how to implement it:

- Step 1—Build Emergency Fund Quickly (page 136)
- Step 2—Pay Off All Consumer Debt Using 2% Rule (page 138)
- Step 3—Set Up Biweekly Mortgage Payments (page 139)
- Step 4—Contribute the Maximum on Your 401(k) for Company Match (page 139)
- Step 5—Build 3 to 6 Months of Savings (page 139)
- Step 6—Contribute the Remaining Retirement 15% Into a Roth IRA (page 140)
- Step 7—Set Up Your Cash and Percentage-Based Savings Amounts and Add Your Contributions (page 140)
- Step 8—Contribute the Maximum Household Allowance for a Roth IRA (page 140)
- Step 9—Round Mortgage Payments to the Nearest $100 (page 141)
- Step 10—Fund Businesses (page 141)
- Step 11—Pay Extra Towards Mortgage (page 141)
- Step 12—Implement the 7-10 Mortgage Plan (page 142)
- Step 13—Decide Your Next Financial Investments and Steps (page 142)

Keep reading to learn numerous techniques for decreasing expenses and increasing income. We will also help you get off on the right foot by introducing worksheets and communication plans. By completing our worksheets and learning how to communicate clearly with your spouse and family about finances, you will be primed to use the 2% Rule to your fullest advantage.

Chapter 3

THE REAL COST OF DEBT: UNSECURED LOANS

BY: CASSIE

Obtaining debt is so easy and seems like such a simple and sensible process. The perception is you simply obtain a loan and pay that amount back over time along with a *little extra* as a service fee (interest), or a way of saying thanks to your lender by inconveniencing them out of that money and letting you use it for a time.

Borrowing money is such a common practice that it can't be something unreasonable or something complicated, can it? If the amount of money you were borrowing cost you 10 percent of the amount you are borrowing, would it be reasonable?

What if it cost you 20, 30, 40, 50 or even 100 percent more than you borrowed? Would it seem like a reasonable solution then?

Let's look into this deeper and discuss what debt is costing you in terms of the ACTUAL amount of money. We want to give you a Debt 101 class in these two chapters. It's important to understand these characteristics of debt so that you can see that borrowing money to get ahead is really not all that it is cracked up to be, and in fact, it puts you behind!

When it comes to obtaining a loan or borrowing money—in the most basic frame of reference—you are accumulating one of two types of debt: unsecured loans or secured loans. Every type of borrowed money can fit into these two categories. Unsecured means a loan without real property, like a car or a house, attached as collateral. Secured means the loan does have collateral.

Let's talk about unsecured loans. Unsecured loans are the type of loan that do not have an actual asset used as collateral. Now, don't think that you can't lose assets when defaulting on unsecured loans. Creditors will still sue or garnish or take whatever legal means they can to collect their money. It's just that the money is not earmarked for a specific purchase. It is simply a loan of some sort, whether a student loan, personal loan, a signature loan or even credit cards.

With the exception of many student loans, these types of loans often carry a higher interest rate than that of secured loans due to the fact they are more risky for the lender since it's simply based on your promise that you will pay back the amount.

Credit Cards

While it can be reasonably argued that credit cards can be used like debit cards, allowing consumers to reap many benefits in the form of rewards and points, this is generally not the case for the majority of the population. The temptation is often too great to use them as a mindless option to get what you want or need without having to think where the funds are coming from.

To understand how much a credit card is costing you, it is first important to understand how to calculate the interest on your credit card.

Credit cards operate under the APR, or Annual Percentage Rate rule. This is oddly named because it assumes interest is calculated at an annual rate. But in reality, the interest on credit cards is calculated daily. This is called the DPR, or Daily Periodic Rate. It may also be referred to as PIR or Periodic Interest Rate. To figure out your DPR is not as simple as you think it should be.

Intuitively, when we see an APR of 14.9 percent, we think it's a simple calculation. If a $1,000 balance remained untouched for one year at a 14.9 percent APR, you may assume you would pay $149.00 of interest over the one-year period—$1,000 × 0.149 = $149.00.

However, because credit card interest is being calculated daily, it would actually be $159.60. That's because you figure your daily rate by dividing the APR of 14.9 percent by 365 days a year equaling a DPR of 0.04 percent or $0.40 a day on $1,000 untouched balance.

But that's not all. You are being charged interest at a daily rate not just on your principal balance, but on the actual balance, which includes accrued interest. In other words, you are being charged interest each day on your original balance plus each previous day's interest that has been added into the balance.

This type of interest calculation method is called compound interest. The interests are compounding on top of each other! We like to call it complex interest because, as you can see, it's so complicated.

Minimum Payment Payback

Let's use the $1,000 balance for a little bit longer. Let's do some calculations on this low balance credit card and let's ask, "How long will it take to pay a $1,000 balance at the minimum payment?"

Most bank and credit lenders figure the monthly minimum payment based on 1 to 2 percent of the balance. Believe it or not, a credit card holder with an untouched balance of $1,000 with a 14.9 percent average APR will take a scheduled six and a half years to pay it off when making the minimum 2 percent payment! Six and a half years to pay off $1,000! This results in $571.52 in interest. The cost of this $1,000 was over 57 percent of the amount borrowed.

All of this doesn't even cover the additional costs of credit card debt. Just try being late on that minimum monthly payment and you'll find out exactly what we mean. First, the late fees that start to rack up on your account are astronomical. If you make your $20 minimum monthly payment late, it can result in a $35 to $40 late fee. Late fees are applied to the balance, so additional interest is adding up each subsequent day.

If you pay late a few times, then the cost increases again when they raise your interest rate. For example, a credit card that starts with a seemingly acceptable APR of 10.9 percent could quickly rise to 29.99 percent due to a few late payments. Apply that now to a more realistic credit card balance, like one we had of nearly $8,000, and imagine how much the monthly interest increases. Better yet, let's take a look.

That $8,000 balance had a minimum payment of about $170 which would have resulted in a total interest charge of $2,514 over five years at the original APR of 10.99 percent. Due to us missing a few payments with a monthly late fee of $40.00 each, they increased our APR to 29.99 percent with an increased monthly payment of $240 with a total interest charge of $9,405 over a six year period. As you can see, not only did the amount of interest we owed change (again assuming this would have been paid off using the minimum payments) by nearly $7,000, but now you see we were actually paying more in interest than the value of the original amount of the loan.

Does this start to give you a sense of how much debt can really cost you? These are just the monetary costs. Wait until we share the non-monetary costs of that same debt. It's truly unbelievable how much debt really costs.

Student Loans

Student loans are a tough subject as the current assumption is that student loans are a necessary debt-evil, like a mortgage. While you may not be able to totally forego the need for a student loan, understanding the cost associated may help you to decide that sacrifices like reduced expenses during those college years and additional paid work the student is willing to do may at the very least minimize the loan amount needed by the student.

There are two types of loans that are available to students: subsidized and unsubsidized. The interest of subsidized loans is paid by the U.S. government while the student is in school. Unsubsidized loans build up interest which is added to the loan balance during those years the student is in school.

One source estimates the current student graduates with an average of $37,172 in student loan debt. Let's take a look at the actual cost of those loans over the life of the loan. For simplicity, we will estimate an interest rate of 6 percent with a 1 percent loan fee. To be nice, we will assume the full amount is fully subsidized, meaning the loan value does not increase during the student's school term.

Six months after the student drops below a half-time status, the student loan repayment starts. Given a standard ten-year repayment term on $37,172, the monthly payment would be $416.85. The total of 120 payments × $416.85 gives us a grand total of $50,022. The total cost of the interest on this loan now equals $12,850.

Instead, that student could have applied that $416.85 each month towards other living expenses during those ten years. Even better, that student could have applied an additional $50,022 towards a mortgage and have been that much closer towards having a paid-off house.

How to Fund College
by Alex

I know a bit too well that the student loans I incurred while in college were possibly not needed in full—to the tune of thousands of dollars. Don't get me wrong, I was extremely grateful that my tuition, books, and room and board were all covered by my student loans. But my spending was a bit out of control between pizza, my beverage choices, the weekend parties or the trips that I couldn't pass up to make my college experience the time of my life—all thanks to those loans. Hindsight truly is 20/20, but it sure seems that much of my extra expenses were a bit unnecessary, to say the least.

I contrast this with my wife's aunt who put herself through college without a student loan or even a scholarship covering the majority of her expenses. She worked full time, ate ramen and graduated with honors debt free, meaning she left school without a huge financial burden to stress about paying back.

We're not insinuating that students need to eat ramen or live in a questionable part of town to scrimp every penny towards an education, but if the mindset *were closer to this* instead of the normal party mindset that I had, maybe we wouldn't see a total of $1.3 trillion in student loans.

When my roommate would ask if I wanted pizza who was I to turn it down? Not me and definitely not with a student loan fund check.

Another story from Cassie's family is about her sister. Although she had scholarships to pay for her tuition, she obviously had other living expenses to make it through the year including room and board, books and more. She and her family decided to take a unique approach and delivered phone books for four to five weeks and were able to make approximately $7,000 over that period.

Although her family sacrificed other activities during that time, like sleep and other fun they could have experienced, that additional $7,000 meant she didn't need to apply for a student loan. And just think, this was just over a five-week period. Had she needed to, she could have additionally worked part time or found other income alternatives to keep from needing to take out loans as well.

Personal or Signature Loans

The next category of unsecured debt is Personal or Signature Loans. These are also known as term loans—which mean that you obtain a loan for a set amount of money and for a set time period.

It's difficult to tell you what the average interest rates are for these types of loans as the rates and terms vary greatly based upon where you obtained the loan, the amount of the loan and your credit history. Here's a chart that gives some general rates and term guidelines. We will use this for our calculations to show you just how much personal/signature/term loans cost.

How's Your Credit?	Score Range	Estimated APR
Excellent	720–850	10.94%
Good	690–719	14.56%
Average	630–689	19.84%
Bad	580–629	28.64%
Poor	579 and Below	Unlikely to Qualify

As you can see, the interest rates vary greatly just based on credit worthiness.

For this example, we are going to calculate a $5,000 personal loan with an excellent credit score. Overall, you would end up paying $1,513.75 in interest to borrow this $5,000 with excellent credit.

But what if you have average credit? It's average for a reason, because most people fall in this range. Let's see what $5,000 would cost with an average credit rating. In the case of this loan, you are paying $2,921.48 to borrow $5,000. That's nearly $3,000 to borrow $5,000. Would you pay $3 to borrow $5?

The Business That Took Us Down
by Alex

One of the major sources of our unsecured debt came in the form of a hopeful money-making opportunity. A couple of years into our marriage, our income was eaten up by the payments for our mounting debt. When a friend presented us with a business she had joined, it seemed to be the answer to not only solve our debt problem but feed our spending habit with the success and riches this new business would bring. This business was to become a sales representative for a popular cosmetics company. We jumped in and invested thousands in inventory from the beginning by using unsecured loans. Her manager encouraged this and promised that this inventory would bring quicker success.

Cassie was so driven to climb the ranks that she was soon on track to earn a free car. But this situation only worsened our debt problem. As she moved up the ranks, the amount of debt we accrued just from this one business was insane. If she was seemingly close enough to the team's month-end goal, she would push, beg, plead and call everyone on her team to encourage them to do whatever they could to place just one more order for the month. She would then pad the final order, paying with a credit card, to make up the difference needed to reach her month-end goal.

She was so happy to reach that month-end goal. But to be fair, no amount of commission check she ever earned was able to offset the amount of money she spent to obtain it.

It only got worse. You see, her habit of begging and pleading her team at the end of each month was the pattern demonstrated to her firsthand by her own manager. Months before, her manager had begged and pleaded with her each and every month even before Cassie was at that point herself. Cassie always felt like it was her responsibility to order as much as she could, as she didn't want to be personally responsible for her manager not meeting her goals and rank each month. Never mind the fact that Cassie didn't have the orders from customers to reflect it or the fact that she already had tons of product from the initial investment and months of orders already on hand. Cassie still ordered to help her.

After several months of this process, each month diving further into debt, Cassie was the proud recipient of a brand new car that she had earned while getting closer and closer to the rank of Director she so highly coveted.

Cassie was living under the false hope and promise that once she achieved certain positions in her business she would be rolling in the dough, driving a free car and having more financial freedom than ever. Instead, when Cassie got there, she was rolling in the debt, driving her adding-to-our-debt car and in more financial despair than we ever imagined.

To get to that point, Cassie had gone into over ten thousand dollars of debt, worked about 80 hours each week and was shunned by family and friends as they were afraid she would attempt to sell them more product or beg them to be on her team. Yet, it was all supposed to be worth it.

Cassie also had this car she had *earned*. We calculate that she actually drove this car for free for maybe about two months. You see, Cassie also had to maintain a personal and team production minimum to continue to drive this car she had earned.

We had decided in order to begin paying down our debt we had to stop going into debt. This included Cassie no longer purchasing product at month's end simply to meet her minimum requirements. So she stopped.

The rules of the company were that if you didn't meet the requirements, your agreement was that you would pay that month's lease, to the tune of $400 a month. During this part of our story, we were already in the red monthly and 60, 90 or even 120 days late on most of our bills. We could not add $400 more to our monthly spending.

So once it got to the point that we were paying that $400 monthly, Cassie told them she no longer wanted the car. A couple of short months later, they picked up the car at an "inopportune" time (see page 55).

I tell you this story not to say that these home-based businesses are a bad idea. If we had truly grown this business honestly, on real sales and the real sales of her team, and not based on Cassie and her team buying the product each month just to move up the ranks, it might have worked, but it would have been harder and at a much slower pace. We would advise anyone going into a home-based direct sales business to run it as a business, and not buy your way up the ranks and certainly not go into debt for this type of business model.

We would also encourage you that if you cannot fund and start this type of a business with cash, we would advise against joining or starting until you can. There is no reason these businesses can't operate debt free. Start with cash, then pay yourself after meeting your business needs and don't go into debt.

Payday Loans

We've shown you just how expensive a $1,000 credit card balance with an average interest rate can be, and it's awful and painful to think about.

But that's not even the worst of it. The payday loan is a special type of debt nightmare where the loan is short-term (generally 14 days) with a fee you might see in a mobster movie.

That might sound a bit far-fetched and extreme, but unfortunately we know this because it was part of our story. When we were getting toward the end of our debt journey, we learned the hard way that the only thing worse than very non-optimal loans with extremely high percentage rates was the payday loan. And, even worse than that is the title loan.

As the most basic definition, a payday loan is an emergency loan that is charged at a super high interest rate, based on the promise that when your paycheck arrives, you will be paying it in full. In fact, the promise is sealed with a special signature . . . on a check. Yes, you write a postdated check for your full balance, plus the interest. So whether you are ready or not, they will cash the check in 14 days.

These types of loans usually consist of smaller balances of $500 or less, with an average two-week term (until your next paycheck). You will also hear them referred to as cash advance loans.

These loans operate differently than most. There's basically a set fee for you to borrow money that is paid via post-dated check at the time you take out the loan.

The cost of a payday loan

Let's look at the cost of taking out a $300 payday loan. For this example, we will use the fees collected by the very same business we went to just over 13 years ago. The rates they were charging then have gone up slightly; instead of the $20 per $100 as it cost us then, the new amount is $25 per every $100 borrowed.

Don't forget these fees are over a 2-week (14-day) period. So let's break down how this loan works.

Using the example of the $300 loan that we originally took out, you simply walk into the business and write them a check for $375, postdated two weeks out. In return, they hand you $300 in cash. You can do this online as well now instead and have the money deposited into a checking account. They are making it as easy as you want it.

When you do the math, that results in a 651.8 percent interest rate. In a world where a 24.99 percent interest rate for a credit card seems gouging, the interest rate for the payday loan is 26 times higher!

But here's the kicker, unfortunately one we know too well. After that two-week period is over, if for some reason you are not able to pay that balance back in full, all you need to do is go back in with another $75 cash (the $25 per $100 borrowed fee) and they will gladly extend the loan for another two weeks.

Maybe you can see just how terrible this situation quickly becomes:

Biweekly Fee	Cumulative Fee	Total Cost If Paid By End of Period
$75.00	$75.00	$375.00
$75.00	$150.00	$450.00
$75.00	$225.00	$525.00
$75.00	$300.00	$600.00

It's almost a bit crazy to say, but all a person needs to do is wait to pay the loan off until the end of four cycles and all of a sudden the fees after eight total weeks equals the amount borrowed in the first place.

Unfortunately, according to one source, the average debtor is in debt for 212 days with a total fee amount much larger than the original amount, as you could probably expect just from the breakdown above.

We didn't quite reach the 212 days, but it took us about four or five loan cycles before we were able to pay it off. As you can see from the breakdown above, we learned the hard way that this type of loan, while seeming innocuous at first, can quickly build up and work against you.

Title Loans

Title loans are a little different, but essentially the same. It is another form of emergency loan, but in this case you give them your car's title. Do you know what that means? If you happen to actually own a car outright, you just handed the ownership over to someone else.

But that's not enough of an explanation. You hand them your title, and they will give you a loan based on a percentage of how much they think your car is worth. This is a high-percentage rate, short-term loan, with a 30-day loan average, with an interest rate generally slightly lower than a payday loan. That being said, the interest rate is still triple digits with the caveat that missed payments could result in repossession of your car.

These loans are scary. For one, they are much like the payday loans as you can get caught up in the cycle each 15 to 30 days by paying the interest on the loan amount and agreeing to new fees and interest for another loan term. But even worse is the fear of losing your car. Different studies have been conducted on those taking out title loans with one such study showing as many as one out of every five title loans results in repossession of the car.

Let's Be Real Here
by Alex

It is VERY easy to get trapped in payday and title loans. Generally, the reason for obtaining this type of loan in the first place is because you can't pay your bills. So you run to a place like this with 600+ percent average APR and you are now caught in a vicious cycle where you still can't afford your bills, and you continue diving deeper and deeper into debt by obtaining these loans.

Trust us. We know what we are talking about, and we know how it feels. We turned to payday loans towards the end of our financial crisis, right before our final options were bankruptcy or let's do something about this! We know how the cycle works. Did you also catch that we said payday loans, not title loans? We did not own a single car at that point, so we couldn't even qualify for a title loan.

These loans are like throwing a brick to someone who is already drowning! Even explaining to you how these loans work brings back so much stress. As these words are flying off our fingers, our heart rates are increasing, our stress-o-meter is reaching high again because, although this was over 13 years ago, it was a terrifying financial place to be in, void of any hope.

We hope and pray that you are reading this book now before you have had to turn to payday loans or title loans. But if you have had to go there, don't worry—you can get out. It won't be easy. We know how you are feeling, how you are coping and how you are feeling ashamed, embarrassed and silently stressed like no one else.

In fact to this day, the baggage that came with the experience of getting caught in the payday loan cycle is so real, that when there is a business we visit next to a payday or title loan business, we will park as far away as we can so we don't have to look at it (or even have others think we are going to it). We hate to think back on that time of our lives or even remind ourselves how dark, hopeless and disparaging that time was for us.

For those, like us, that have had to use one or both of these sources for emergency money, you probably already know how much they cost. It is like selling your firstborn.

For those that haven't used these sources, let us tell you, plead with you not to go down that route, or better yet, don't get yourself so financially strapped that this becomes your only option.

Even in the midst of that, we were able to find a way out, and we hope that no matter where you are financially, you can see there is hope. Even when it seems so dark and when it seems like there's nowhere else you can turn, there is hope.

The Total Cost Of Debt

Remember when we asked at the beginning of this chapter if a loan were to cost you 10 percent of the total value, would it be worth it? Or what if it cost you 20, 30, 40 or upwards of 100 percent more than you borrowed? Would it seem like a reasonable solution then? We hope you see now how each of these debts by themselves cost much more than you likely anticipated. But let's take a step back and consider an even more amazing view—the total cost of your debts.

When we started our debt payoff process, we calculated our total monthly interest as well as the time it would take to pay it off with minimum payments. We discovered we were paying over $1,200 in interest each month with an estimated payoff of 64 years paying the minimum. We're not sure about you, but this totally shook us to the core.

As you continue reading, don't just consider the cost of each loan, but consider the bigger picture. That just might give you the motivation you need to get started with this plan and to stick to it.

Chapter 4

The Real Cost Of Debt: Secured Loans

By: Cassie

Secured loans are the type of loans where there is an actual asset, or collateral, attached to the loan, meaning that you are borrowing money for a specific purpose like a car or a home. It also means that if you default or don't pay your monthly loan amount, your asset can be taken as collateral with the result you lose that property due to non-payment.

Because there is an actual asset attached to secured loans as collateral, it generally means a lower interest rate, as it's slightly less risk for a lender. However, don't think that this means you are getting away with borrowing a lot of money for a very little payback cost. Just keep reading and you will find out how much that debt is costing you.

Vehicle Loans

How much does an auto loan cost you? Let's take a look at the costs and fees associated with a $20,000 car loan to see how much that car will actually cost you.

We will start at the lower end of the scale for car loans with a rate of 2.9 percent and the average time period of six years (72 months). The monthly payment for this loan would be $302.98 for a total of $21,814.53 paid over the life of the loan. That means that in the six years you are paying on the vehicle, you are paying an extra $1,814.53.

What if instead you were only able to qualify at a higher average interest rate of 8.9 percent over six years? The difference in the total payment is extraordinary! The monthly payment for this new loan would be $359.52 with a total of $25,885.36 paid over the life of the loan. With this vehicle loan, you would be spending an extra $5,885.36—a significant 25 percent more than the amount originally financed! Are you happy paying 25 percent more for a vehicle?

We Got Smarter

In our debt-laden past, we had some impulsive car buying experiences that led to financial woes that you will read about soon. However, because of our 2% Rule, the last vehicle we bought on credit was paid off three years early (therefore saving some of that interest we would have paid) and we owned it outright for over 7 years of the 11 years we drove it. When it was time for Alex to get a new commuter car, just this past year, we bought a car that was five years old, a reliable brand with a higher gas efficiency. We paid 40 percent of the price of a brand new vehicle, received a super deal and a little more because we could hand over actual cash. It was the most amazing feeling and we drove away with very little paperwork, with the title arriving in the mail a few days later and no car payment! This was the best car buying experience to date!

Mortgages

Now let's take a moment to look at mortgage loans.

According to Census.gov, the median home price is $284,000 and the average home price is $353,600.

Let's base our calculations on the median home prices. We are going to use the median as we believe this is more accurate according to what the average American would be buying. The median price is the middle price of homes sold—meaning half cost less than this and half cost more.

The average prices are determined by the sales prices of all homes divided by the number of homes sold. That means that the handful of multi-million dollar homes included in this figure greatly inflate the actual average American home price.

In addition to the actual median home price, we will also show calculations on a lower-priced home, to illustrate how much that lower-priced home is actually costing you as well.

First up, the median home price of $284,000 with the average 30-year loan rate at 4.5 percent.

Mortgage Repayment Summary—30 Year Loan Term		
$1,438.99 Monthly Payment	**$234,035.06** Total Interest Paid	**$518,035.06** Total of 360 Payments

Over the course of 30 years, this home will actually cost you an additional $234,035.06 for a total of over $518,000. This is 182 percent of the original home's cost!

What about a loan with a 15-year term at the lower interest rate of 3.75 percent? Shorter is MUCH better as you are taking half the time to pay it off which means fewer interest payments, and in general, the interest rate is also lower. As we see below however, it will still cost you a pretty penny!

Mortgage Repayment Summary—15 Year Loan Term		
$2,065.31 Monthly Payment	**$87,756.11** Total Interest Paid	**$371,756.11** Total of 180 Payments

In this case, the same $284,000 home will cost you an additional $87,756.11 of interest with a grand total that is 131 percent of the original home's value. As you can see, the shorter term with a lower interest rate resulted in a lower total cost, but the total interest is still high.

Let's share the rates on a much lower-priced home for the sake of comparison, a home at $190,000 at 4.5 percent for a 30-year term first:

Mortgage Repayment Summary—30 Year Loan Term		
$962.70 Monthly Payment	**$156,572.75** Total Interest Paid	**$346,572.75** Total of 360 Payments

The cost of this home would actually be $156,572.75 more. Again with a total out-of-pocket expense of about 182 percent more than the original cost of the home.

Finally, we must show the same home on a 15-year loan with a lower interest rate of 3.75 percent.

Mortgage Repayment Summary—15 Year Loan Term		
$1381.72 Monthly Payment	**$158,710.08** Total Interest Paid	**$248,710.08** Total of 180 Payments

This $190,000 home will end up costing $58,710.08 more, for a total of 131 percent of the original home's value.

We wanted to show these figures to put into perspective what debt actually costs you. Keep in mind, car loans and mortgages are considered by many to be "good debts."

Real Car Costs Part 1

We look back on our lives and wish that for one second we would have understood how much a car loan really costs. In fact, our hands-on experience with car buying is far beyond a simple misunderstanding. We previously understood that credit and debt were the only ways to buy cars.

It's a bit of a shock now, looking back and realizing that this was our perspective, as both sets of our parents were very conservative car buyers. They bought older, used vehicles, perhaps making some car repairs here and there and driving them into the ground. They did not believe in driving something they couldn't afford, or being thoughtless about car purchases. Yet, somehow we both walked away from our childhood homes thinking the opposite about cars.

Alex came into our marriage with an old truck that he bought for $1 from a friend. After investing $600 in DIY repairs, he drove that truck for a number of years. I came into the marriage with an old reliable and sturdy Buick that drove perfectly. My parents gave it to me when I turned 16, free and clear with no payments and no debt. I owned it outright and really had not put any major work at any time into it.

We owned two vehicles. OWNED. Looking back, we really can't pinpoint why we were not content with two decently reliable vehicles. Not only were we not content, but we were unhappy that we had these vehicles.

Then one night. . . .

Alex was driving home on a snowy winter evening when the old Buick sputtered to a stop. Strangely enough the only open facility on this road was a used car lot.

His initial thought was that he would use their phone to get help in towing our old car to the shop. But as you could guess with our story, it didn't end up that way.

In fact, as he marched toward the car lot with the intention of using the phone, thoughts started like, "Maybe this was a sign? Maybe this exact scenario was exactly what we needed to buy something more reliable."

Alex rationalized the situation by thinking that it was irresponsible to have an old car that was less reliable. If this car had broken down that night, who's to say it wouldn't happen again?

Seriously, what are the odds of a car breaking down and the only business in sight that was open was a used car lot, and they happened to be having a sale and happened to have the exact make and model of a car that Alex had been eyeing and dreaming of in previous months?

The scenario made it so easy to justify the need for a new used car, especially with Alex's mental state in those moments. How do I know that? Because he did make a call like he was going to originally, but the intent of the call was different. He called me to lay out his scenario for a new used car!

Unfortunately, the call was an easy one because my mindset was already at the "I need a new used car" point. I justified it by thinking that buying a new, gently used car with financing was a smart purchase because it wasn't a new car that lost much of its value soon after driving off the lot.

Honestly, neither of us thought about how it might be wise to first determine the issue with the Buick before committing to buying a car. All that mattered was that we bought that car. That night. With their financing. Without even a second thought. Oddly enough, the car repair for that old Buick wasn't all that much. It was a very minor problem requiring a minor repair, so I continued to drive it and Alex replaced his truck with this new car.

Shortly after, reality started setting in, but not a responsible reality. It was the reality that Alex got a new used car, and I was still stuck with this old Buick. I had a professional job, too, and I needed a professional image to portray to my employer, to my friends, to my family and to everyone around me that didn't even know me. We just assumed that if you drove a nice vehicle, you were doing well.

This time we were going to be smart. We were going to negotiate and get the best deal we could. We would still buy used, because as long as you buy used, you are getting a great value and therefore it is a responsible purchase.

During one intense moment when the salesman walked away to talk to the manager, Alex placed his hand on my knee and said the most chilling thing.

"Cassie, you know that if we get this car, you can't quit your job? Without your job, we can't afford this car." The REAL truth was we still couldn't afford it with my job. Then he got a little irritated and said, "Cassie, what I am trying to say is that if we get this car and then we end up having a baby, you can't stay home. You'd have to keep working."

I knew what he was saying the whole time. I just didn't want to think about it. I looked at him in the eye and said, "I know!" As if to say, "I don't care."

That short, 20-second conversation was one of the most extensive conversations we had had about money in our marriage to that point. It was one that still is eerily haunting to think about today, because it was just another nail in the coffin. Not a nail really, but a bolt that was screwed down so tightly, it couldn't be released with any ease.

We walked away with that "new to us," gently used car and traded in that old Buick.

That conversation was forgotten and our hole of debt dug just a little deeper.

So let us take the time now to point out that our $108,000 of debt did not include our mortgage. This was separate. Dumping the consumer debts, basically everything except the mortgage, should be a primary financial focus. Then, in Chapter 18, we will show you how you can pay off your mortgage in 7 to 10 years without blood, sweat and tears after setting the financial post-consumer-debt stage.

The purpose of touching on mortgage loan costs here is to paint the picture of what debt actually costs you. Remember, these numbers are not meant to frustrate you, but to give you hope about what's to come in your financial future when you apply the method and principles we are sharing. Just think about how your financial world can open up without these interest costs!

Even though it is not counted in the story of our accumulation of $108,000 of debt, if you must know, consistent with our track record of the first several years of our marriage, we had a terrible time with real estate as well.

We bought our first house, which in and of itself wasn't a terrible purchase. It would have been much better had we paid cash and if we had known about our future 7–10 mortgage plan. I'd like to say we would have applied it, but at that moment in our lives, responsible debt-free living was not on our radar.

The loan officer pre-approved us for a home up to $225,000. Thankfully, we didn't jump all in, completely stupid at that point. When we personally looked at our budget, we knew that a $225,000 mortgage was going to cause great emotional and financial stress. The math that home lenders apply is a one-size-fits-all scenario.

Instead, we decided to look for a house under $100,000. At this point, one year into our marriage, we had the maxed-out wedding credit card, the honeymoon credit line that we were very quickly spending, a car loan for Alex's vehicle and student loans. With all that, we wanted our payment under $900 a month. Don't forget this was 15 years ago, in a small town in Idaho, so it's hard to even think about homes under $100,000 now. We had found a perfect starter home, only eight years old, perfect for many years for a potentially growing family. It was a split entry with four bedrooms, two bathrooms, 1800 square feet and a double-car garage with a fully fenced backyard and fully finished basement all for $88,000. Yes, I miss that house. We received a decent rate for that time and a good deal. We put $0 down, but the sellers paid our closing costs.

So what happened? After living in our home for 1½ years, Alex was on the verge of losing his job because his company was only a couple of weeks away from closing its doors in the small town where we lived.

He was the *only employee* offered an alternative.

Now mind you, this was after we had been living in our home for 1½ years. In that time, we had racked close to $70,000 of total consumer debt.

What was Alex's job alternative? A move to another state. They would even pay $2,000 of our moving expenses.

It was a scary time. Since we had only been in our home for 1½ years, we probably couldn't make any profit when considering the cost to sell our home.

We had no additional money. We were already $70,000 in debt. That $2,000 was generous, but not quite enough to cover a move of that extent.

However, the alternative to not moving was a job loss in a slow economy, and because of our financial woes, this was a complete no-brainer. In fact, since it was the same company, just an office in another state, there would be no lapse in pay. That was the only comfort. We were already at the point where a week or two without pay could put us over the edge.

Alex was told about the job option on a Thursday. If he wanted it, he would need to start work on that following Monday.

He took the job. He had become good friends with one of the guys that worked there. This friend offered to let Alex live in his house with his family until I could sell the house and move so that we didn't have a mortgage AND rent at the same time. We will be forever indebted to this family for this blessing. They had no idea how much they saved us! I don't know what we would have done!

We did sell our house quickly, within two weeks in fact! So by the time we closed and it was all said and done, we were officially moving six weeks after he started his job.

However, in the process of selling, moving and settling, we lost money on our house. We sold it for $90,000, but we really hadn't paid off much of the original $88,000. By the time we paid the realtors and our closing costs along with the closing costs of the buyer we lost about $5,000. By lost, I mean $5,000 further in debt for a total of $75,000.

We tried to find affordable housing or something equivalent to our prior home. The cost of living was much higher where we had moved. We couldn't afford to live in this new state. Alex did receive a slight boost in income, but not a lot. We looked at homes for sale by owner that were of similar style, size and type of home we had in Idaho. They were literally double—yes, you read that right—DOUBLE the price! The exact same type of home was now $165,000. We knew we couldn't afford it.

Instead, we found some small, cute cottage-style homes around $100,000 with detached single-car garages. They were newer, but very small and quaint. We figured this was the only thing we could buy, but we were wrong. The mortgage broker laughed at us when they pulled our credit in an attempt to get us pre-approved—in sum, we couldn't. Our income did not add up to our debt load and our credit was in the low 500s. It was bad.

We couldn't buy anything. It didn't matter if it was $10,000, there was no way we could buy a home.

This still wasn't enough to shake us to our core and make us acknowledge the cost of our debts.

The next step was to look for rentals or apartments. The problem was we had pets: two small dogs and two cats. Between our four, furry family members and our credit score, we scared all potential landlords away.

We were homeless. We had nowhere we could live. We had one final option: a trailer.

A software engineer and his wife were homeless. HOMELESS.

The trailer was our only remaining option. We found a decent park with newer trailers. We didn't know if they would even accept us. The way this option works is that you buy the trailer and then you pay rent to the trailer park for the lot your trailer sat on.

First, we had to be approved to buy the home. Our credit was bad, bad I tell you! But they agreed to sell us a trailer if we could put 10 percent down. They agreed to take a risk if we could give them this cash in hand within a few days. The problem was we had nothing. We had maxed out all of our cards, we could not get another loan at the time, and so we did the only thing we could: we took $5,000 out of our retirement. Here we were in our mid-twenties and already needing to take money out of retirement, which of course resulted in a penalty and a high tax rate due to early withdrawal.

We showed up a couple of days later with a magical $5,000 in hand to give to the lender holding the loan for the trailer. The next obstacle was being approved by the park. They actually accepted us. They didn't seem to think it would be a problem.

We moved into the only place we could live. We were happy to have a warm bed, shelter and a place to call home after that arduous shake-up in our lives.

We lived there for 4½ years. I was able to get a job in our new state shortly after finding a place to live. It was a good job, and so that just meant we had a bit more clout to obtain more debt over the next year.

It was during our time in this trailer that we accumulated the rest of our $108,000 in consumer debt. This was where we finally woke up to our financial despair and woke up to our "Why."

Real Car Costs Part II

Jump ahead four years after our first set of car purchasing and financing errors. We were now expecting our second child. We felt that we needed to become a minivan family. At this point, we were about a year into following classic cut everything out debt-reduction plans and the two steps forward, one step back success, or lack thereof.

The car we purchased, or rather financed, four years previously was not paid off. I still had three years on the loan, but going from a family of three to a family of four seemed to necessitate the need for an upgrade to minivan. The real truth was that I hated my current car for what it represented. I was bitter, embarrassed and disappointed in myself with every mile I drove that car. I wanted yet another excuse to get something else so I could get rid of my guilt, my immature buying decisions and put it behind me. Besides, in our current debt payoff plan, this car made no sense. I had to get rid of it.

It was a car that we could not afford. All of the debt-reducing experts tell you to sell and get rid of vehicles that you cannot afford. This car fit that category. In our minds, upgrading to a minivan, since we would need one anyway soon, was the best way to get rid of it.

We spent hours again in the dealership. Our credit was completely in the toilet at this point. Even though we had stopped all credit card spending and were making progress, our credit score was still bad because we were still in the early stages of attempting to pay off our debts.

And still, in our minds, buying a car on credit with a loan was not that bad a financial decision.

I cannot even remember how bad our credit was exactly, from our best memory it was somewhere between 480 and 510. We shouldn't have been approved for any loan amount, at least at a reasonable rate. In fact, the initial lenders were offering us loan options in the low 20 percent range. To this day, we still have no idea how, but a last offer came in from a credit union having pity on us and approved us for a loan with an interest rate of less than 10 percent.

It wasn't just that. The salesman made us feel we were getting the deal of a lifetime, especially in light of them doing us such a favor. It was even recommended by the salesman at the time that we shouldn't even hesitate at jumping at the deal. Had we been buying the van with cash and without any additional stipulations, they just might have been right. But there was more to the story as we still owed money on my current car and couldn't afford an *additional* car payment.

So for the deal, we had to trade in my car that we still owed money on. What did they give us for it? Well, they paid off the car loan for me, but what that really meant was that the amount I still owed on the current car was added to our new minivan loan, tacking on several thousand more dollars to the actual price of the van. Yes, we traded it in. But by their appraisal, the car was worth much less than we owed, thus the reason for the balance being tacked onto the new minivan loan. Now considering the additional balance from the previous car, the high interest rate and the actual cost of the minivan, that minivan wasn't such a great deal after all.

Other Costs You Don't Consider
by Alex

As you can tell, debt of all kinds comes with significant cost. But there are other costs we often either deny or don't realize as true costs of debt.

One such example occurred just a short few years after we had moved out of state for my job. We were already nearing an unmanageable debt-to-income ratio, and just a few weeks of going without a paycheck would spell certain bankruptcy.

Around that same time, my prior boss called me one day and asked if I would have a chance to stop by his office for an interview; he was the director for a new startup company, knew I was in the area and really wanted me to come work for them.

In many ways, it was a dream come true. It was honestly a position that I couldn't turn down, as the skills I would acquire would carry over to other software development jobs, and the startup had a lot of promise due to both the investors backing the business and the companies they were already supporting with their new product.

Though it was a position I couldn't turn down, I had to. There was just no way I could financially afford to make that risky move, no matter how good that new position would be.

But it was even more than that. Not only could I not go without a check, I also knew the reality of working for a startup. I was working for a stable company at the time and knew that taking a risk could put us into a situation where unemployment was a reality if the company fell apart.

As you could guess, that company saw huge success in a short time, even receiving an award from the state for being one of the most innovative companies. Sure, they could have failed, but in this case they didn't. It makes me sick to my stomach that I missed out on an opportunity to work for a company that really took off. I could be in a much higher position today—I missed out on that dream job of a lifetime.

I honestly can't put a dollar price tag on any of this, but missed opportunities will always have a price associated even if you cannot quantify it.

Missed opportunities are not just in the shape of missed jobs. Maybe you can look back over your own life and see missed opportunities of all kinds. They might take the form of missed investments that you really wish you had the money for, or missed risks at work that you couldn't imagine taking because you really needed to keep your job. What I mean is that sometimes you become a yes-person because you don't have enough stability to take risks when you want.

This doesn't even mention the other costs that aren't even financial. The stress and strain our massive amount of debt placed on our marriage was almost overwhelming. Not only was our marriage suffering, but so was our health.

Chapter 5

Our Mother's Day And Finding Your Own Why

By: Cassie

Are you ready to get started and see real differences start to happen in your financial life? Are you ready to get out of debt, to actually own your home, save for retirement like never before and be free of the financial burden of owing others money? Are you even ready to have peace in this aspect of your life so you can stop worrying and enjoy the rest of your life?

That's awesome and we're excited to walk along with you as you make those changes! But we need to ask you a question that might seem on the surface a bit primary and unrelated to getting started on this process of meeting your financial goals.

Our question to you is, "What is your why?"

What we mean by this is what is your deepest and most intimate reason for moving forward with this plan and starting on your journey towards financial freedom?

We encourage you to find the answer to that question to prepare you for when the going gets tough or when time seems to be moving so slowly as you work towards your financial goals. Sure, you might start strong and even get through the first few months of seeing the changes to your finances, but you're going to get to a point when you need to keep going even when you don't want to.

We can tell you right now that it is going to take a great amount of determination, motivation and desire to make changes big or small in your financial situation. It's at that moment that it's so critical that your "why" will take over and keep you going, even when you don't want to anymore.

The silly thing is we hadn't identified reasons for our "why" to motivate us in our finances until we were at a desperately low point in our lives. That "why" didn't develop when we were financially strapped and could no longer live the lifestyle we had previously enjoyed those first few years of marriage. No, losing that lifestyle wasn't enough. It wasn't developed even when we were juggling bills and playing the game of, "Well this one is only 30 days behind and this one is 60 days behind, so I guess we should pay the 60-day late bill." And it didn't even develop from the incessant phone calls from bill collectors demanding payment right then or even the collection letters that caused us to develop our "why." No, none of that really motivated us.

Perhaps much of it was that no one asked us what it would take to get us started on a debt-payoff journey, and we certainly did not ask ourselves the question because we didn't want to change our ways at that time of our lives. The idiom "what you don't know can't hurt you" proved untrue in this case. The opposite is resoundingly true!

Our hope as you read this book is that you will think about your why right now, not wait until times become desperate. Develop a why and let it be your motivating factor.

Our "why" came in a much more dramatic way. Maybe because we needed something bigger and more drastic to wake us up. Our "why" was starting to be developed on one very providential morning in May many years ago. In fact, it was Mother's Day. Our "why" started early one morning as I lay in my bed not wanting to face another cold, lifeless day. My mind was exhausted, my body was exhausted, our finances were exhausted, our bank account was exhausted, our credit scores were exhausted, our credit cards were exhausted. But our creditors were definitely not exhausted as they just seemed to build more steam to come after us each and every month.

But that Mother's Day, it wasn't the creditors, our bank account, our credit scores or the fact that we had nothing to show for it that provided the glaring moment when we finally had enough motivation to begin a debt payoff journey.

That Mother's Day I discovered I was pregnant.

This is where our "why" came.

We wanted to get out of debt so we could fulfill the dream of having a family, raising kids and me being a stay-at-home mom. All things that were currently unreachable given our extreme debt. But we now knew we needed to try, to strive to get there no matter the struggle it would take. And because we found our "why," we had exactly what we needed to get started, and more importantly, to finish our journey of paying off that debt.

As you read our story, you may or may not be able to relate. But one thing we want to be very clear about is what is it in your life that motivates you. Simply stating, "I want to get out of debt," is likely not to be enough.

You need to find what shakes you to your core, what obstacles are in the way of your hopes and dreams and define these in a very clear and real way. You need to have those tough conversations with your spouse, kids and family before it feels like it is too late.

What would have happened if we didn't have a positive pregnancy test that month? I honestly do not know. Would it have been something else that would have kicked us in the behind to get to work on paying off this debt? I don't know. But what I do know is that no one had challenged us to find a reason and perhaps if someone was there to ask, "Why do you want to be debt free and have a bright financial future," we very well could have been on this journey much before this desperate point.

That's why we are challenging you now!

The Pregnancy Test That Started It All

I began screaming with pure joy and excitement.

Alex immediately jumped up out of bed to join the party while I waved that familiar stick around and screamed. He too was screaming.

We held each other tight, tears flooding down our faces. As we both stood there holding onto each other, Alex stopped and said, "Happy Mother's Day, darling."

Oh, the tears and the sudden joy were overfilling me like nothing had before. It was the most emotional day of my life.

That first night my emotions were so intense. I was elated, yet so scared. This was real life. This was happening, whether we were ready or not. In less than eight months, we'd be welcoming a new baby into our lives.

I lay there with my mind racing. I was so confused. I was scared, I was mad and I was bitter . . . already.

What could possibly be wrong at this time in my life? What could be the ONE thing to destroy it all! The secrets we brushed off, suppressed and hid from family and friends for years about our financial disaster. We looked like we had it together on the outside. Now, I was carrying this precious, precious life and gift from God and our lousy choices that led to a life of poverty were no longer going to affect just the two of us. It was going to affect the life of a child that did nothing to deserve this lot in life.

How could we be so short-sighted? Immature? Stupid?

We were in debt. Not just a little bit. Not just a lot. But a whole lot of consumer debt . . . to the tune of six figures in consumer debt.

SIX FIGURES in debt.

We were sunk. I couldn't be that stay-at-home mom that I wanted to be. I would forever be in debt, working day in and day out to pay it off, missing my child, and missing the life I wanted.

I looked over at Alex who was sleeping so peacefully. I was furious at him. But we didn't talk about it. We never talked about it. We hadn't talked about it up to this point, and so why would we talk about it now? It seemed like not talking about our debts was the answer. It seemed reasonable if creditors gave us more loans, if they thought we could handle it, then why shouldn't we be able to handle it?

I finally fell asleep crying and praying. I felt enough peace to finally close my eyes and rest. When I woke the next morning, I was ready to figure this out. If this is what we wanted, surely we could figure out how to get through this.

Alex woke with a smile on his face. I didn't want to crush his elated fatherhood dreams the very second he awoke. However, I knew we had to have this adult conversation soon.

The next day, I had the day off. It was a weird day. Overjoyed and filled with blissful tears, I called friends and family to share the good news after many years of dealing with infertility. These phone calls became depressing as the comments of, "Oh, I am so, so excited! You finally get to be that stay-at-home mom!" were repeated. I had shared these dreams with them. They knew this was what I wanted, but it felt like my friends and family were being spiteful, even hateful by pressing that question so much. How could they say such hurtful things to me?

But they didn't know. Only Alex and I knew the truth. We were not well off, we were not doing fine, and I was very far from any position of being able to stay home with my child.

As much as I wanted to celebrate the growing life inside of me by eating out, like we always did when there was any excuse to celebrate something, that didn't seem right in these moments. I scrounged around the kitchen and made a home-cooked meal. I seemed to be such a novice, yet this is what I wanted to do full time?

I had dinner ready before he came home. I didn't want any open window for him to say, "Let's go grab a bite to celebrate at the steakhouse!"

After we indulged in a little small talk, in nearly the same breath, we both blurted out, "We need to talk." We both knew what the other was going to say and what the other was thinking. It was relieving on one hand, but terrifying to finally have a conversation we should have had a long, long time ago.

Alex spoke first. He admitted that this had been plaguing him for so, so long. I interjected and said, "Me too!"

In the course of our uncomfortable, yet necessary discussion, we discovered why we had never had this conversation before. Neither one of us wanted to be the killer of joy. Neither one of us wanted to grow up. Neither wanted to be the one to say, "Hey, we can't take this trip. We can't buy these shoes. We can't go out to eat . . ."

It felt unloving, cruel and perhaps just cold to say "no" to each other.

Well, what were we going to do now? This is where we grew up, and we grew up fast. We had debts looming over us, and not just looming over us, but literally knocking on our door. We had found our "why," our reason to finally grow up and get out of debt.

Communication Is The Key

As we started to work on our debt, we would continue to fail in our plans until the communication became more open, intentional and regular between us regarding our finances. Then one day we realized our communication had improved, with the result of better success in our debt payoff strategy.

We will be talking about important aspects of communication for everyone: single, married, married with kids or whatever your situation may be. Even if you are single and doing this on your own, your communication with friends and family around you is just as critical for you as it is for anyone else in the process.

In those early days of our marriage our communication in the area of finances was in the toilet. Remember, neither one of us wanted to be the bad guy when it came to spending money. How do you not be the bad guy? You keep your mouth shut!

The ironic part of all of this is that from day one, people knew we communicated well. In fact, many of our close friends and family accused us of over-communicating. I know, weird, right? In many regards, they were right and at the same time, dead wrong.

You see, we talked to each other multiple times a day, and it drove our friends and family nuts. In many cases this would seem normal for two young people in love who wanted to share every detail of their lives with each other. But the elephant in the room was that we did not talk about setting up a budget, controlling spending or halting the debt accrual, not even once! So when it came to the grown-up subject of money, we didn't communicate when it counted.

Our money talks went something more like this:

Cassie: "Wouldn't it be nice to go on vacation next month?"

Alex: "Yes, that would be fun. We should plan it. Why don't you find us a deal, and let's get it booked."

Cassie: "Great, I'm on it."

The next day after discussing every detail concerning travel, hotel and even options along the way:

Cassie: "I'm so excited to be going on vacation next month!"

Alex: "Me too!"

Sure, somewhere in the process we might say, "Well, this hotel is $100 more per night, we'd be fine staying at this hotel that is $100 cheaper," kind of money talks. We thought that not going all out like we did on our honeymoon was being responsible.

So, before proceeding any further you need to ensure you are communicating well with everyone that is important in this journey: yourself, your spouse, your children, extended family and your close friends. This might sound like a lot, but your communication needs to be on the right track, or else your efforts will be in vain, and you will be spinning your wheels and becoming very frustrated, very quickly.

Communication with self

"Communicating with yourself?" you ask? Yes, the first person to talk to is yourself. You have to be the first one convinced that you can and will do this. You are the first person that can cut you down, be in denial and trick you into not even trying.

You can also be the first person to motivate yourself, to encourage yourself and to give it all you've got. If you are not convinced you can do this, you will not be able to do it, nor will you be able to encourage anyone in your family, especially your spouse.

Communication with your spouse

If you are married, this is crucial. It is not really possible to be in a marriage with one spouse committed to a goal and the other not. That's why getting on the same page with your spouse is the next step to properly communicating about finances.

This is a touchy subject. We have met spouses who are both eager to start and both ready and willing to do whatever is needed to get it done. We've met couples where one is committed and one is indifferent. We've also met couples where one is diligently trying and the other does the opposite.

How do you move forward if you have a spouse who is not very excited about your desire to be debt free or to be at a better place financially?

We offer the same advice for all couples and it has worked in nearly every case. We will talk about those rare cases where it hasn't worked further into this chapter.

How to open the lines of financial communication

For many, simply saying, "Hey babe, I want to talk about our financial future. Let's do this together and make a plan," is enough. The subject just may need to be brought up and both spouses could be excited and eager to finally get on the same page.

Regardless, we are going to encourage everyone to take a step-by-step approach with their spouse. For some, as you implement these steps, one of the biggest things we can tell you is to approach your spouse with grace, love and humility. It's not a time to make accusations, threats or point out failures. This will do more damage than good.

Yes, it may be a trying and emotional time for you, but if your spouse is less attuned to the financial situation than you, they will be more emotional and sensitive about money. If you want to change your financial situation, and you are the one that has the initial desire, then you are the one that needs to have the initial conversation and start it off on a positive, loving, helpful note! Keep this attitude in mind as you continue working through this book.

- Step 1—Tell your spouse that you have been very stressed and worried about the finances, and you know that you haven't handled the money and finances very well yourself. You are worried about the future and want to move into a more secure and stable future.
- Step 2—Ask your spouse if they would be willing to share their goals, hopes, dreams and desires for the near future and long-term future so that you can both make wise decisions about the finances and be on the same page and to encourage and love one another along in the process.
- Step 3—Fill out the questionnaire about finances (see next page). Set a time in which you will turn these into each other to review privately in the next few days.
- Step 4—At the time that you turn these questionnaires in to each other, set a date to go over and discuss each other's questionnaires.
- Step 5—Actually have your meeting in a non-threatening, non-accusatory relaxed setting and really learn to understand how each of you view money, debt and the goals you each have for the future. Open up this communication and try to understand each other like never before.
- Step 6—Taking the goals, hopes, dreams and desires that each of you share, decide on timelines and priorities, and discuss how using the 2% Rule can work towards meeting these goals. Encourage your spouse to read this book to understand the 2% Rule for meeting financial goals and how that can work into your plan!

This is where the 2% Rule works even more beautifully for those reluctant spouses. They very often don't want to give up everything, which is why they don't want to talk about it. Instead, this plan helps you to creatively work together to find these small cuts to meet the goals—instead of saying, "No" constantly and carving a bitter future.

Financial Questionnaire

My top five financial and purchasing priorities.

1. _____
2. _____
3. _____
4. _____
5. _____

If money were no object, what are my top dream goals and wants?

_____
_____

How important are my wants?

_____
_____

What do healthy finances look like to me?

_____
_____

What are the things I value the most?

_____
_____

How do I feel about debt?

_____
_____

Do I want to be debt free? Why or why not?

_____
_____

What are my goals for the next year?

_____

_____

What are my goals for the next five years?

_____

_____

What are my long-term goals?

_____

_____

Do I have any other financial or life goals?

_____

_____

What are my retirement goals (age to retire, desired lifestyle)?

_____

_____

What about those spouses who still refuse to get on board?

Yes, there are some for which the above process still doesn't work. If this is the case, there is perhaps a different problem going on beyond money. There may be a problem in the marriage. This is the point in which counseling is needed.

Once these issues are dealt with, the money issue can come back into play.

Communication with your children

Learning to communicate with your children about money after learning how to communicate with your spouse about the subject will, most likely, be a breeze.

With younger children, there really won't be a lot of communicating other than the basics.

If you have older children and teens, this is going to be a bit trickier because they may be used to a certain lifestyle, certain privileges, certain expectations. After living a life they have known, to come in and pull the rug from underneath them can create some bitter, negative feelings.

That is why a humbling explanation to your older children and teens is probably going to be necessary. The best way that we have discovered for how to bring up the subject with your teen with the news that life will be changing is by you, as the parent, admitting your own failures. Apologize to them and ask your child to forgive you for being a bad example, or for not being as diligent with the finances as you should have been.

Communication with your extended family and close friends

In the beginning of implementing our 2% Rule, we quickly discovered there was a crucial piece to the puzzle in communication—family and friends.

Yes, it became very obvious that keeping them in the dark was not a benefit! We needed their support, too. Why? Well, if your family and close friends have an expectation of you in regards to gift giving, dates, shopping, trips, hanging out and a certain standard has been set, you are probably going to have to change that standard.

It might seem intimidating, or even embarrassing to say, "We can only go out to dinner once this month." Or to tell your extended family, "We are going to be spending less for Christmas." Or, "We need to come up with a different extended family vacation this year." Really anything that involves your friends or family and money needs to be discussed.

It doesn't mean that you can't spend time with them. It just means you need to be more creative in how you spend your time with them.

How do you approach your family and friends on this topic?

Simply call them up or have them over and let them know what is going on, without the need for details. Just tell them, "We are really trying to hit some big financial goals for the next few years, and so we have adjusted our budget so we can meet these goals! But in order to do this, we will need to cut back on various activities."

Then reassure them that you want to spend time with them and find ways that you can still do that on a budget. Although we enjoyed going out with friends for dinner or a night on the town, we ended up developing greater relationships inviting them to our home and having a fun dinner and games in. It gave us more freedom, time and the ability to have a closer relationship! It really was a double blessing by saving money and creating better friendships.

Chapter 6

Two Steps Forward, One Step Back

By: Alex

I wish I could write and tell you that once Cassie and I woke up to the financial crisis we had found ourselves in that our lives were changed and we immediately had clarity of vision and action to implement the perfect strategy to pay off our debt. I wish I could share that our plan from that day forward consisted of a new lifestyle that resulted in a quick and successful debt payoff.

If you've tried to implement a Get Out of Debt Fast solution, I assume you chuckled at that last paragraph. Maybe you rolled your eyes. Possibly you didn't even want to respond because you know from your own experience that it's just not that easy.

Unfortunately, we know just how difficult it is when you start the process. Our first attempt at paying down our debt resulted in us paying down about $15,000 in just over three years.

To even get to the point where we admitted we had a problem, both to ourselves and even later to friends and family, was difficult. Honestly, the phone calls from the creditors were painful and walking into a payday loan office was utterly embarrassing, but this had become our way of life.

Finding out we were expecting our first child finally opened our eyes. The debt issue was no longer one that just affected me, or even me and my wife. Now the issue was affecting our children, including this first child we were going to bring into our lives. How could we bring a child into this situation and in good conscience keep going down this same path we were following?

Repo Man

I'll never forget that cold, blustery day in the early days of our debt payoff plan. Earlier that week, we had brought home the most precious, beautiful child our eyes had ever seen. She was in our arms continuously, and she looked to us as if we were her entire world. The truth is, at that time we were. We were all she had, and her whole future and livelihood were in our hands.

Our pastor had stopped by that day to bring a meal and meet our child. It was during that visit that we received a knock on our door.

When I opened the door, I was immediately rattled back to the reality of our financial situation. Thankfully, we were visiting with our pastor in another part of the house, and it wasn't obvious what was transpiring. The man standing at the door was a tow-truck driver there to take back Cassie's car, the car she had earned through her sales job, but which we could no longer afford to keep.

Seriously! This was going to happen with our pastor, who didn't know our financial situation at our home visiting us and our new child?

I excused myself and tried to nonchalantly handle the repossession as quietly and quickly as I could. We did know it was going to happen. We did have the car cleaned out, and we were just waiting for the tow truck to come, but the timing was impeccable. I mean, we couldn't have found a worse time for him to come.

When I came back into the room nothing was said. To this day I have no idea whether our pastor knew, or just guessed, what had happened, either that day during the visit or later.

After he left, Cassie and I didn't really talk about it either. We quickly acknowledged we were glad to be spared from potential embarrassment.

The reason we share our many failures is because we want you to know that at the beginning of our journey we struggled. We want you to know that we know what it's like to see no light at the end of the tunnel for a long while. We know what it's like to try, to really think we were making progress, only to still fail in our initial steps.

This is where we would like to share some of the reasons we believe we struggled so much in those initial years. You'll note our first reason is just symptomatic of where we started our journey, and debt was just something we had to come to accept. The rest, though, are reasons that we could have and should have overcome. If only we knew then what we know now, how much pain and stagnated progress we could have spared ourselves.

Our goal is to share these with you now so you can learn from our mistakes and keep yourselves from learning from the school of hard knocks like we did.

1. Don't Forget Where You Are Starting

Let me get right to the heart of it. Obviously, we don't know you, the situation you are in now or even where you have been. We know pretty grim circumstances from our own past. We know that everyone is starting under different circumstances.

With that said, there's a good probability that some of you might be starting in a similar, if not darker situation than what we were in. We were months behind on our bills, maybe you are far worse. We did have a job, maybe you don't. But with all of that, my encouragement to you is that it might take a few months to start to feel like you're being successful in managing and paying off your debt.

You probably will still be behind in the initial months, even if you are dedicated in cutting your 2% from expenses and adding your 2% of extra income.

We encourage you to take a breath, allow yourself to see the progress you are actually making, and know that you are on the right path. Allow yourself to see that in just a few months, time you really will get to the point where you just have the normal monthly bills.

You can do it! And you will!

That is, if you don't stop or quit because you think there is no hope or it's no use trying. You just need to remember that the hole you are digging yourself out of might require just a bit of grit at first to get to a point where you can breathe.

2. Not Communicating Was A HUGE Mistake

Communication is one of the most important keys in reaching your financial goals. The flipside of this—not communicating honestly—sets you up for failure.

Cassie and I were actually accused of overly communicating early in our marriage. We just loved to talk to one another about everything, except for some darker subjects that we didn't want to talk about, like finances.

We might talk about a trip, or an event and make huge plans. We would even discuss different ways that we would save and pinch pennies to be able to do it all for less. But questions on whether we should even be doing it in the first place, whether we should be paying down a loan instead or a past-due balance, were not topics we discussed. It's almost like we didn't want to know.

Communication is a key you can't forget when it comes to your finances. We believe lack of communication is a result of a few simple reasons.

Sometimes reality hurts

This is often a huge contributor to lack of communication whether in a marriage or any other relationship. Sometimes the discussions that have to happen are those that are painful. The sooner you start addressing the communication problem and become united with your spouse on a solution, the quicker and potentially less painful the resolution will be.

We don't want to be told that something is unwise

I know this sounds odd, especially when talking to another adult about whether or not we should spend money on a certain item or event. In the end, it can be easier to hide an event or spending question from your spouse because you already know what the answer should be, and you desire the immediate pleasure of having what you want over the financial consequences of spending that money.

We're afraid that our spending plan will be less important than someone else's

This really ties into the last issue but is a bit more specific. There are times that each spouse can have a disagreement over whose spending request has a higher priority. Cassie and I both had our specific requests, but it wasn't until we sat down to address wants and needs that were we able to start moving forward.

Again, this partly goes back to the fact that we often already know what the best course of action is, we just don't want to admit it.

We want to deny there is a problem and instead live in our dream world

In the end often we just want to pretend that everything is OK and that nothing is wrong. I know Cassie and I often dealt with this. After getting our loan on our honeymoon, it became so easy to forget the fact that we were in a terribly embarrassing situation, instead telling ourselves we were going to experience and enjoy our dream honeymoon.

3. Not Understanding Our Spending Weaknesses

Along with struggling with communication problems, we failed to take the time to understand our weaknesses. Honestly, this would have been resolved had we communicated more thoroughly, and if we had been more mature in our relationship, both to one another and even to our financial situation.

Without realizing or even discussing our weaknesses, it was easy to continue down a path that resulted in the same problems we had before.

Addressing Our Weaknesses

Cassie had a weakness for travel. During her childhood, her family traveled all over the nation. As such, she found any excuse she could to travel and enjoy a trip, and I was easily convinced.

I had a weakness for eating out. During my childhood, my family enjoyed local restaurants and making life easier by allowing someone else to prepare our meals. All Cassie would have to do is mention how tired she was after a long day of work, and it was more than enough to get me to spring at the chance to grab a quick bite to eat.

In those early years of paying off our debt, we struggled. Not understanding each other's weaknesses made it easy to continue the old spending habits even when we knew we shouldn't.

Once we acknowledged my weakness was eating out, we found that having meal options at home took away those easy excuses. We also found joy in taking the time together to share in the preparation of a meal as part of our Date Night In. We could share a gourmet meal that we prepared together and ate at home, all the while filling that desire for a treat or meal that I craved so badly. Even today, some of our favorite dates are when we find an exquisite menu and prepare it together, sharing our lives with one another and just relishing each other's presence.

As for Cassie's desire for travel, we found ways to enjoy ourselves by pretending to be tourists in our own city or even having very occasional nights out to enjoy some of the same pleasures, but in a much cheaper option.

As time goes on you'll find it easier to overcome some of these weaknesses, but especially early on in the financial journey it helps to identify those weaknesses so you can know how to manage them.

You'll find that once you understand each other's weaknesses, you will know each other better. I know this may sound trite, but the combination of the vulnerability of sharing those weaknesses with one another, coming up with ideas on how to help one another through those challenges, and ultimately encouraging one another can really help you build a closer relationship together, although it seems painful at the start.

4. Trying To Use The Crash Diet Approach

Unfortunately, there is one more large reason we were so utterly unsuccessful those first months and ultimately the first three years of our first-round attempt to become debt free. It all stems from a process that people often use to conquer problems in many areas of their lives, which is the crash diet approach towards paying off debt.

When standing at the checkout, how many magazines do you see with articles promising that you can lose 15 pounds the very first week following this newly discovered diet? The very next week, that same magazine will have another headline sensationalizing the fact that this person just lost 85 pounds in just over a month using yet another fad diet.

What's sad is that so many people who are buying into crash diets will be hurt time and time again because they won't see the same astounding results. One of the largest reasons for disappointment is that those diets are unsustainable. Even if you do see the weight come off, once you go back to your normal lifestyle you gain all that weight back and usually more.

For many of you this crash diet approach might seem a little crazy. But honestly many people take the same type of approach when it comes to their budget. What took years to acquire will suddenly be resolved by slashing your budget by 75 to 80 percent? The goal is to make short-term sacrifices on this crash diet plan to get out of that debt.

Just like those fad weight loss diets, the majority of people that start a crash debt-payoff approach unfortunately never see the touted results. Whether they keep slashing to the point that they keep falling off the wagon each month or just get to a point that it seems too painful and overly taxing to live under that type of bondage, they just stop and wait for another day and another debt-payoff plan that will solve all their problems.

However, there's another side of this that needs to be addressed. Maybe there are those that successfully follow this drastic approach and pay off their debts. As they go back to living life per their normal lifestyle, they soon find themselves on the path right back to where they started before, back into the debt they just paid off.

We have friends that have admitted that they did successfully become debt free using popular plans, but even now they are using it again to get out of debt for their third or fourth time. The problem is that instead of making small, gradual changes to their lifestyle that become sustainable, they are making drastic cuts that can only be maintained for brief intervals.

We share this here because we tried using this crash diet approach when we first started to pay off our debt. It was this crash diet approach that crashed our budget each and every month we tried.

We happened upon a popular crash-diet, get-out-of-debt-fast approach, and we were fired up to get going! We were ready! We set out committed to implementing this new lifestyle and this new plan. We had to first set our new budget. The idea was to set a budget on the minimum bare bones that you can live on. We were hearing about those families that sacrificed so much in the short term, eating rice and beans now to live their dream life later. It sounds harsh to live with such tight constraints, but the idea was a temporary sacrifice for long-term gain. Once you were out of debt, you could go back to your former lifestyle. You could go back to eating out, you could go back to getting your nails done, you could go back to all of those luxuries.

Honestly, that should have been our first red flag. What is the point if we live like paupers one day and princes the next? We should have seen that this led to a vicious cycle of getting out of debt over and over again.

But we didn't. We worked diligently on that first budget. We went through all our bills and slashed our expenses like no one else. We wouldn't eat out anymore and we would live on rice and beans—a 75 to 80 percent slash in our budget. Oh yes, we were proud of that document and the life we had planned on paper that would solve all our problems.

The next few days were grand. We were eating all our meals at home. I was either coming home for lunch or taking leftovers the next day, and we were surprisingly living within that extremely tight budget. That is, until . . .

I'm not sure what it was. It might have been that we were out later than we had hoped running errands, or maybe I had just come home late, and we had another commitment that night. Whatever it was, we went out to eat, and in one failed attempt, we blew our proposed budget for that month. There was no going back, no way to resolve it. Our budget was just so perfect and so tight with the result that one failed meal out made us immediately fail the whole budget.

So we did what any other self-respecting person would do. We resolved that we would try again next month . . . only to find ourselves repeating much of the same scenario month after month.

Why crash diets and crash debt plans fail

Do you recognize this at all? I'm not just talking about in respect to finances. This is the identical story of attempting a crash diet for weight loss that fails time and time again. You either start the diet and quickly fail due to your expectations being too unrealistic, or you successfully complete the diet, but find yourself gaining those pounds back within weeks or months of losing them. What was the same result we mentioned? Failure.

This is where we struggled over and over again in those first three years using that crash-diet approach to only pay off $15,000 of our debt. Some months were more successful than others, but generally they all had a similar result—not reaching perfection, not living according to the budget of our dreams, and then promising that we would try again next month.

As time pressed forward we discovered a few principles that we would use to morph a crash-diet approach into the more gradual approach we present instead in this book.

Crash diets set you up for failure

There's something about a crash-diet approach that tends to result in failure a majority of the time. Historically, it's believed that up to 95 percent of attempts at a crash diet resulted in regained weight. Only a small percentage of people actually achieved long-term success. No matter what you believe about that statistic, whether you're someone that has tried this approach to weight loss or even have friends that have used the same approach only to fail, you probably know from those experiences that this statistic is unfortunately closer to reality than we all want to admit.

What is it about this approach that results in such an astounding failure rate?

The goals of the crash diet are built on the ideal

Do you recall what we just said earlier in this chapter about our first approach to budgeting? We worked hard scouring over our bills, our expenses and our income to try to come up with the most ideal budget that anyone could develop for our situation.

We knew that we could live on the barest necessities for a short time if it meant having huge results in finding debt freedom. The issue is that that budget was based on ideals that we could never realistically attain. When we said that we cut our budget by 75 to 80 percent, we're not making that up. Especially in the food market, we determined that we would never eat out, that we would only buy those items that would guarantee the lowest possible expenses.

All it took was one failure, one time missing the mark of the ideal that would keep us from meeting that month's budget. We found that when you try to live too unrealistically you easily set yourself up for failure. The principle we learned through this process is that trying to cut too deeply and too unrealistically really was unrealistic.

Instead, as time marched on, we learned that a more gradual approach towards cutting your budget can actually result in a more realistic plan that can result in a successful implementation, meaning a much higher chance of success in meeting your long-term goals.

This type of lifestyle is not sustainable in the long term

Not once did we ever think that the lifestyle of short-term sacrifice would be something we could sustain or keep doing for the long term. In fact, these experts kept reminding us that these were temporary sacrifices for long-term gain, and we would get our lifestyle back once we were debt free.

But herein lies part of the problem with this approach. When your goal is short-term sacrifice and you never retrain yourself or your family on what life will be like after that sacrifice is accomplished, eventually you get back to what you were doing before you started this plan and usually find yourself back into much of the same debt you were just trying to pay off a few short months earlier. Again, this goes back to our friends trying to pay off their debts for the third or fourth time using this same type of approach.

But what if you had a different approach? For example, what if instead of going straight for the ramen and other unpleasantries, you were to find creative ways to cook for your family that were healthier, cheaper and ultimately ways you could sustain long term?

Those small gradual changes will eventually become a part of your family's lifestyle. Instead of dreading that huge cut to your budget, it just becomes a part of how you conduct business in your home. Maybe you can see how once you pay off that debt you're not going back to an old lifestyle, but instead just living life as you've now trained yourself to live.

Chapter 7

Putting The Plan In Motion
By: Alex

Implementing The 2% Rule

In Chapter 2 we introduced the 2% Rule, which was critical in our success at climbing slowly and steadily out of debt, and has since led to our increased financial security. Here's a reminder of the six steps you will follow to implement the 2% Rule:

1. Track your expenses and earnings for a month
2. Create your baseline budget based on the results from step 1
3. Decrease spending the following month by 2 percent
4. Increase income the following month by 2 percent
5. Apply the "found money" from steps 3 and 4 towards your financial goals
6. Each month repeat steps 3 through 5

Remember, you are not pulling an unrealistic budget out of thin air, and you are not creating an 80 percent reduction in spending. You are using the actual amounts spent and earned in a month to create the goals for the following month.

Also, don't forget that communication is a major key to success, even if you are single and working this out by yourself. If you haven't filled out the Financial Questionnaire on page 51, make sure you do that before starting the process.

Decreasing Your Expenses

You're going to see throughout this process that you will be inwardly prioritizing how important certain expenses are to you, then evaluating which ones to cut. Maybe your family likes to eat out, and potentially even eat out a lot. I mention this first because that's where we started. Unfortunately, we loved to eat out, and our debt had a lot to show for that. But once you realize you're only cutting 2 percent, you can see that you don't have to cut all your eating out. Instead you could maybe only cut out a meal or two per month. It's honestly crazy how quickly one or two times dining out can add up!

Perhaps you already are super frugal, and you just don't know how you can squeeze another penny out. Well, that is great, and it is a fun place to be because then you get the fun game of really challenging yourself each month! There may not be much you can do to decrease at this point, but don't worry—the plan is not one sided. The other piece of the 2% Rule, increasing your income, has no ceiling, so you will still get ahead of where you are now.

Perhaps you are a massive spender at the moment. If that is the case, you will easily decide where to challenge yourself and your family to cut 2 percent from your budget, and you will probably be able to do this for many months before hitting your rock-bottom budget.

Chances are, you are probably somewhere between the two extremes. You will still have a good number of months where you can play the game and find ways to cut 2 percent each month.

When you start this 2 percent decrease plan, you will go through a few phases:

- Phase 1: This is a piece of cake—I can cut 2 percent all day. Our warning to you is don't be tempted to over cut, as you will quickly frustrate yourself! You are EASING into a smart money lifestyle for long-term success that you can live on sustainably.
- Phase 2: "It's beginning to get a bit more difficult"—I love the challenge of trying to figure out where I am going to get my 2 percent decrease this month.
- Phase 3: "The challenge is real"—I am diving into a deep challenge and pushing myself and my family to a whole other dimension as I creatively squeeze 2 percent out.
- Phase 4: "Not quite 2 percent but I can still find little successes here and there"—I have played the game and played it well. I can't find a 2 percent cut anywhere, but I did find a $10 cut here and maybe another $2 there.

Once you reach phase 4, you are at your rock-bottom budget.

Don't stress and fret if a month pops up and kids' new uniforms, school materials, an unexpected date night out or anything else happens. The joy of this plan is that you are succeeding, and you are not going to let yourself get beat down. At each phase, you will have extra money left over each month and potentially a lot of it. If unexpected expenses pop up for a month, it simply means you may not be putting as much down towards your debt or your savings for that one month. Remember to plan for expenses that may be coming up ahead of time to try to eliminate those surprises.

The point is to always be challenging yourself, reaping the benefits of that extra money each month and enjoy living a little more financially free than you did the month before.

What you'll find as you move forward is that sometimes it's not a matter of cutting an expense but rather finding a more cost-effective way of achieving the same outcome. You might even find your family living better than you ever imagined for much less than you imagined as well.

How do we know this? We live on less now as a family of eight than we did as a married couple without children back when we were racking up our debt. In case you're wondering, we are using the tips we share in later chapters to buy healthier options for our family as well. We promise you don't have to live on macaroni and cheese or other processed foods to meet your budget. It is almost like eating your cake and having it too—just the opposite way around.

A Tip On Where To Start

First, we recommend reviewing your actual budget again. Look at your records again closely. Did you see it? Often there's a charge we like to refer to as a "head smack charge": that monthly fee that you've been paying without realizing it for a product you signed up for months ago that you don't use. Maybe it's even a couple of head smack charges.

These might include an educational charge you signed up for that you haven't used for a few months. Maybe it's a digital streaming product that you haven't used, or only use once a month. Of course, maybe your family will see more value in paying that small amount with the goal of cutting your cable provider.

Sometimes these charges will make up the full 2 percent cut for the first month. If so, then you've made your plan, and you can carry on with the intention of meeting that goal by month end.

However, if you still need to cut more to meet your 2 percent goal for the month, we encourage you to start looking at other items in your budget. Maybe you don't have any of those charges remaining to cut, but you do have other charges you really don't care about as much anymore.

Quick Tips
Just a few ideas you might want to consider for the first few months:
- Decrease the number of times you eat out at restaurants (see Chapter 12 for more tips)
- Save money on your meat purchases (see Chapter 13 for more tips)
- Learn the tricks of the trade on decreasing your grocery budget (see Chapter 13 for more on that)
- Cut your electricity bill (see Chapter 11)

Increasing Your Income

This is probably the most misunderstood part of our plan. First, we are not saying is that you need to walk into your boss's office and demand 2 percent more hours per month or even a 2 percent bonus each month instead. In fact, in all the years we've followed this plan and taught this concept, not once have we ever had anyone demand a raise from their boss. I guess it if it works for you, then congratulations!

Instead we are talking about something totally separate from your day job. We will be digging into this later, but the goal here is to get you brainstorming on ways your family can creatively take some time together and combine all their skills and talents to find a way to generate extra income each month.

At first, this might be a part-time, low-paying job to initially start bringing in some extra money. In fact, we started by delivering newspapers after our oldest daughter was born.

But then we got smarter.

After looking at our separate skills, we were able to first find more lucrative jobs: Alex doing contract software development and Cassie teaching coupon classes. Later we combined our skills to start our website, The Thrifty Couple. As time has passed, we've started a number of other websites and other business ventures as we try to leverage our skills.

Moving Forward

Now of course we're assuming you set out with these goals and you plan to meet them with 100 percent success. But, we also know that life happens. Whatever your goals are, this next month just might not turn out the way you had hoped. The best part of this plan is that it's flexible. You won't be getting months behind in your goals and wanting to quit because of it. Instead, you'll just pick up where you are and move forward.

What if your results were even better than expected? Amazing question and a great problem to have! This just provides you additional money to apply towards your goal. Plus, the following month's plan will be a gradual, 2 percent better.

So let's talk about that next step now.

Chapter 8

The Exponential Payoff Strategy

By: Cassie

With the goal of paying off over six figures of consumer debts, we developed our 2% Rule and made slow, gradual changes. Those changes ultimately led to a lifestyle of wise financial choices. We succeeded in cutting our budget for many months until we hit our rock-bottom budget and created a surprising lifestyle of increasing our income successfully month after month.

These two sides of our 2% Rule created a perfect harmony of success in paying off our debt. It created a sustainable lifestyle that not only would prevent us from going back into debt, but would also allow us to continue as we progressed toward our next financial goal!

The funny thing is that when you think about 2 percent, you automatically wonder whether such a small amount could really pay off nearly $100,000 of debts. I know, it's crazy to think about! To this day, even though we did it and still implement these concepts today, it's hard to believe that such a miniscule change each month could result in such a monumental financial impact for our family. So, yes, we paid it off!

What It's Like Today

Today, we are a family of eight. We live on much less, and we live better as a family of eight than we did when it was just the two of us those first four years before we had any children.

It's difficult to find evidence today of what that $108,000 of debt bought us. In fact, most of what we spent it on was gone in a flash, gone in an instant, forgotten and useless.

But the pain of it has lasted our lifetimes. It still affects us today emotionally, especially when we consider how much further along we would be today if we hadn't needed to pay off all of that debt and lose all of that money to pay interest. It's not a situation that we want to see anyone get into.

The freedom of being debt free has been incredible. We can take business risks and thus see success we never dreamed of. We have the freedom to freely give more to our church, community and organizations that are helping others in very real ways. It's such a gift to be able to put these things first!

Being debt free has taught our family the meaning of contentment, of working hard for something you want, of planning ahead and of being intentional with our money. We hope it will lead into a life of financial peace for our children in their future.

As for our marriage and relationship, well, money is no longer an issue. We are on the same page and don't argue about money. We see our plan clearly, we see our needs versus our wants clearly and we are considerate of each other's hopes and dreams, while being considerate of our budget. We are also realistic and respectful towards one another and allow ourselves room for encouragement from each other without getting offended or upset because we know we need that accountability. We communicate about money and communicate on a very intimate level. We intentionally keep the money topics a safe and open discussion.

Small Changes Have An Exponential Impact

Did you know that if you fold a sheet of paper 43 times, it will reach the moon? Yes, if you could fold a piece of paper 43 times, you would reach the moon about 240,000 miles away. It's baffling when you think of this piece of paper, less then 0.05 mm thick—it doesn't sound possible. But when you do the math, the reality that this piece of paper could get you to the moon with these "small changes" gives you a whole new perspective! Indeed, these "small changes" have an exponential impact.

Our 2% Rule is based on a similar concept, with simple and achievable guidelines. Although our plan probably won't get you to the moon, you will be elated with peace, joy and contentment each month when you see amazing progress, progress that may appear now as an unbelievable goal.

That's where our deep-in-debt to debt-free story comes together.

As we started that first month with our 2% Rule—with over $90,000 left to pay off—we put our feet to the ground to find our first 2 percent cut and bring in that 2 percent income increase. That first month, we had over $200 extra to work with. The next month, this increased by 4 percent

(2 percent decrease and 2 percent increase) to equal $208 extra. We kept this momentum rolling each month, doing a total of at least 4 percent (2 percent decrease and 2 percent increase) better each month.

We often made an excess of 2 percent increase of income each month, which we applied to our debt. In addition, as we paid off debts we applied those payments to other debts. The momentum builds quickly once you stop paying late fees and exorbitant interest rates.

Our Strategy For Rapid Payoff

We wanted to consider both interest rates and balances when it came to prioritizing our debts.

After discovering just how much we were paying in interest each month, we really wanted to knock out those high interest debts first. At the same time, the more cash we had to throw at it, the faster it would decrease as well. That is why we discovered the best way to determine the order of payoff was to create a simple prioritization.

Step 1: Use The Full Debt Overview Worksheet To List All Your Debts

Filling in this worksheet lays out the reality of the loan balances, interest rates, time frame (at minimum payments) and whether the payments are fixed or adjustable for all your outstanding debt. You can use online calculators to determine lifetime interest and minimum payment payoff times in months.

For this process, we created the Full Debt Overview Worksheet.

Full Debt Overview—*Tip: Record all of your debts, including credit cards, credit lines, automobiles, student loans, etc. This is the fact-collecting process to help you open your eyes to your total debt load.*

Debt	Monthly Payment	Interest Rate	Lifetime Interest	Balance	Minimum Payment Payoff Time	Fixed or Adjustable Payment

Here's an example for a sample family:

Full Debt Overview						
Debt	Monthly Payment	Interest Rate	Lifetime Interest	Balance	Minimum Payment Payoff Time	Fixed or Adjustable Payment
VISA CC #1	$98	17.9	$5723.04	$4,200	256 months	Adj.
Car Loan (Suburban)	$297	3.25	$1696	$12,300	28 months	Fixed
Credit Line Bank	$345	14.75	$10,188	$8,500	30 months	Adj.
VISA CC #2	$155	22	$10,056	$6,200	58 months	Adj.
Student Loan	$90	1.5	$620	$9,000	108 months	Fixed
Unsecured Loan	$45	18.9	$737	$649	17 months	Adj.
VISA CC #3	$37	12.39	$1249	$1,050	34 months	Adj.
Car Loan (Kia)	$189	2.95	$491	$3,895	22 months	Fixed

Once you have all your debts identified in this high-level view, it allows you to make easier decisions on how to prioritize your payoff. Our easy and effective solution for deciding what to pay down first takes into account both the balance and the interest rate as identified in the following steps.

Step 2: Use The Overview Of Debt Payoff Plan To Group Your Debt

Overview of Debt Payoff Plan—*Tip: Determine priority in each group based on balance, interest rate and payment amount. The more cash you can find available in a short amount of time, the faster the overall payoff.*

Debt	Interest Rate	Balance	Priority	Goal Payoff Date	Monthly Payment
$0–$1,500					
___	___	___	___	___	___
___	___	___	___	___	___
___	___	___	___	___	___
$1,501– $5,000					
___	___	___	___	___	___
___	___	___	___	___	___
___	___	___	___	___	___
$5,001– $10,000					
___	___	___	___	___	___
___	___	___	___	___	___
___	___	___	___	___	___
>$10,000					
___	___	___	___	___	___
___	___	___	___	___	___
___	___	___	___	___	___

Use this Overview of Debt Payoff Plan to prioritize your debts by grouping them according to the following balance categories:

$0 to $1,500

$1,501 to $5,000

$5,001 to $10,000

Over $10,000

Step 3: Within Each Category, Prioritize Your Debt Payoff Plan

There are a few things to consider when creating your debt prioritization plan. These are the criteria we recommend, but evaluate these as a family and decide if a different prioritization would work better for you. Assign a priority within each balance category to determine payoff order using the considerations below.

Consideration #1: Initially organize the debts in each balance category from highest to lowest interest rate

Because the debts in each category are close to the same balance, you can see that at this point it probably makes the most sense to pay off debts with the highest interest rate first. That way, as the balance comes down each month, there will be much less interest charged against that balance.

This consideration is probably the most important of all and at the very least should be your starting point. You can see an example of this in the priortization of balance category $0–$1,500 on page 72.

Consideration #2: Consider paying adjustable monthly payment debts first prior to fixed payment debts within each balance category

After ordering by interest rate, you might want to take a second pass to review whether it would make sense to pay off adjustable payment debts like credit cards and credit lines first to give you that extra boost of encouragement when you see the minimum payment go down drastically each month.

That in and of itself might be reason enough to slightly adjust the order of payoff of the debts within a certain category. This consideration is represented in the sample balance category $1,501–$5,000 in which the VISA is both a higher interest rate and an adjustable loan.

Consideration #3: Prioritize student loans last because the interest is a tax write-off, and they are deferrable in case of job loss

Having the interest as a tax write-off is honestly a small reason for pushing these loans down in the debt payoff priority. The greater reason is that if something were to happen to your primary income source, you can seek deferment of those student loans until you regain employment. Finally, because the interest rates are usually not as high as other debts, they will probably wind up lower in priority of payoff anyway.

See an example of this in the balance catagory >$10,000 where the student loan is prioritized last.

Debt	Interest Rate	Balance	Priority	Goal Payoff Date	Monthly Payment
$0–$1,500					
VISA CC #3	12.39	$1,050	#2	_____	$37
Unsecured Loan	18.9	$649	#1	_____	$45
_____	_____	_____	_____	_____	_____
$1,501–$5,000					
Car loan (KIA)	2.95	$3,895	#2	_____	$189
VISA CC #1	17.9	$4,200	#1	_____	$98
_____	_____	_____	_____	_____	_____
$5,001–$10,000					
Credit Line Bank	14.75	$8,500	#2	_____	$345
VISA CC #2	22	$6,200	#1	_____	$155
_____	_____	_____	_____	_____	_____
>$10,000					
Car Loan (Suburban)	3.25	$12,300	#1	_____	$297
Student Loan	1.5	$9,000	#2	_____	$90
_____	_____	_____	_____	_____	_____

Step 4: Determine A Rough Debt Payoff Goal To Estimate When Loans Could Be Paid Off

After determining the payoff prioritization, you can then start with the first debt in the lowest balance category and make an estimation, which becomes your goal to meet or beat, as to when you can pay off this debt.

To figure this estimation, use the following steps:

- Start with the minimum payment
- Add in the projected excess you have left over each month after paying all your other bills
- Add the money saved from your 2 percent spending decrease
- Add the additional income coming from your projected 2 percent income increase

Each of these amounts will add together to help you determine how much you will be paying towards that debt each month. Then, divide the total amount of the loan balance by this amount to help you see how many months, in your estimation, it will take to pay off this debt. Don't worry, this is just a rough estimation to help you set goals to meet or beat.

Then, to figure the second debt in that category, follow the steps above, plus add in the full monthly payment amount you are rolling over that you were paying towards the last debt that you just planned to pay off.

So in this example, the second debt priority (remember in the first balance category) would be determined by adding the excess left over after paying all the bills and budgeted living expenses, along with the continued 2 percent spending decrease and 2 percent income increase and now the additional $45 from the loan just paid off.

After completing the estimation for this second debt, then repeat the process for all the remaining debts listed. As we hope is obvious, each subsequent debt payoff plan should include the amounts you were paying from *all* previous debts scheduled for payoff.

You are rolling the payments from all the previous debts forward when you attack each subsequent debt. And we love the word attack, because you really are waging war against your debt and winning battle after battle.

After reading this process it might sound daunting. However, once you start calculating and working through it, it becomes addicting as this defines your goals along the way. You will want to calculate it to the end as it will give you hope and vision not only of *when* you will be done with it, but that you actually *WILL* be done with it!

It was really an amazing process to be a part of and to watch when we went through this ourselves. It was so encouraging to see these debts destined for one, two, three or even six decades of minimum payments scheduled to be completely gone in a few months time!

The $50,000 Year

The last year of our debt payoff, we were dumping $3,500 to $4,500 a month into our debts! This was a combination of our excess after bills and living expenses, the current month's 2 percent decrease and 2 percent increase, and the rollover payments from all the previous balances of all the previous debts.

At first we were paying $1,200 a month just in interest. When we had eliminated more than half of this, plus the principal payments from the previous debts, it created a nice monthly excess amount to throw at the next debt.

The first year, we paid off about $15,000, with most of that happening towards the end of the year. The second year we paid off around $25,000 or $2,000 a month. In the last year, we paid off nearly half of the $90,000 that we still owed. This is what happens. You have a gradual increase each month with huge balloon payments at the end because all of those gradual changes from early in the process add up.

You just can't give up!

If someone had told me when we started this process we would have been paying $4,500 off in debt each month that last year, I would have assumed we had won the lottery at a payout of $4,500 per month. Otherwise, this didn't seem possible!

But that's the beauty of it! It might seem like a slow start at first, but this process compounds quickly, painlessly and effectively!

That first year, our slow start of paying off $15,000 turned out to be much easier in comparison to the $15,000 paid off over three years of false-start crash diets prior to our 2% Rule.

Other Steps To Aid In The Process
Negotiate interest rates

Yes, we made many calls over the years of our debt-payoff plan in an attempt to negotiate our interest rates. Many calls were unsuccessful, but some were successful and just saved us that much more time in payoff and cost of the loan.

This is our process for negotiating interest rates:

- Be a good customer—In order to have success in dropping interest rates, your best bet is to be in a really good position, meaning you have paid the bill on time for a number of consecutive months. They want to know that you are a reliable debtor. If so, you can often reduce your interest rates as a reward for your good credit behavior. This automatically lowers your payments.

- When you call be VERY NICE—They do not have to do anything in response to your request. It is still your debt and obligation regardless of what the interest rate is on your debt. But being nice always gives you a leg up. You are at their mercy, and you need to act like it.

- Know exactly what you can do—Can you apply a several hundred dollar lump sum payment right then in exchange for a lower interest rate?

- Whatever is arranged, be sure to ask for it in writing—Get the name and number of the representative, the date, the summary of the conversation, and then ask for an email or mail confirmation. Be sure it is finalized and done before you hang up.

- If they can't help you now, ask when they can help you and what you need to do for the future—If they just are not willing to negotiate at this time, simply find out when you will be eligible or what you can do to have better success next time. Most of the time, they will be honest and tell you their requirement. Then plan to work towards these things and call in the future when you've met these requirements.

Please note, we are talking about negotiating interest rates, not balances.

Negotiating credit balances usually means that you will receive dire credit consequences. Rarely is there a balance negotiation that does not negatively impact your credit score. In some cases it can be just as bad as bankruptcy. Don't forget that will stay on your credit record for seven years. So you need to seriously consider the consequences before trying to settle your debts for less than you actually owe.

Boost debt payoff with tax refunds

We boosted our debt payoffs by immediately dumping any tax refund we received into the next debt on our priority list. We didn't tempt ourselves by celebrating with dinner out or by making other major purchases. Retailers really feed off people by luring them to make large purchases using a tax refund during tax season. We didn't keep it in our account long enough to be tempted. It went into the account and back out the same day!

This boost was also a huge encouragement to us by seeing those balances drop even faster and with such an amazing result.

Stick with the 2% Rule

We just want to emphasize again how our plan and process is a simple solution—the simple steps shown above.

We hope this shows you that you don't need to take drastic measures in most cases. Our situation was pretty dire, and we didn't do anything extreme to pay it off, but we followed the scalable and easy 2% Rule each month, we were intentional, and we followed our debt-payoff order.

How To Handle Medical Debts

There are circumstances and situations that arise where it seems the only solution is to pay off medical debts with a credit card. We advise that you do whatever you need to do to pay off your medical bills without acquiring additional consumer debts.

Doctors, hospitals and medical complexes may sound threatening, like they need you to pay now or else, but in reality if you are paying something to them, they likely won't pursue further legal action against you. The BEST thing to do is to be in constant and pleasant communication with your medical debtors. Work out a payment plan at the lowest possible monthly payment, especially for those that don't charge interest, to give you the most flexibility in paying down your other debt.

As you negotiate with them, you can ask what the lowest possible payment could be, communicating with them your intent to pay more as you have money available. As you get close to paying your balance, try to save up a chunk of the balance. When you have all of the balance available, ask to talk to a manager and negotiate your final balance if you were to pay in full right then. We did have a number of medical debts and generally found that we were able to receive a 20 percent discount on the remaining balance of those debts using this approach.

Let's emphasize this scenario with an illustration. Suppose you have a $2,000 medical bill. Generally, a medical creditor is going to want you to pay it off in a few months. This may not be possible. You negotiate with them that you will pay $50 a month, and you make this clear that this is all you can afford at this time. They may not be happy with you on the phone, but they will be happy to receive a $50 monthly payment for three years instead of a legal fight.

Let's say you are two years into your consistent $50 monthly payment (or occasionally more) medical debt and now have a balance of $800. Assume you can apply $550 to the medical bill TODAY. Call them and ask to speak with a manager. Tell them, "I have been consistently paying $50 a month on this bill for 2 years. I have $550 that I can send to you today if we can call the balance paid in full. Can we do this?" Often, the medical debtor will accept or at least come back with another offer, like if you pay $600, so be sure to have a little more to work with. Then they will write-off the rest. BE SURE TO REQUEST A RECEIPT and a statement that shows paid in full. We have done this many times with successful results.

If they do not accept your terms, don't tie up $550 or $600 of your cash in paying off that debt. Just keep paying the $50 monthly payment by politely saying you'll just continue making your monthly minimum payments.

Other Ideas To Aid In Your Process
Sell expensive cars and downgrade.

This is not a popular approach, as most people don't want to give up things they love and have worked hard for. But, let's be honest, if you bought a car that you cannot afford, you haven't worked for it. Perhaps you will be working for it the next five to seven years, but is this car worth all of those years of hard work and sacrificing other things in life? Wouldn't the freedom of being debt free be worth more now?

When we did get serious about paying off our debts, we saw that we could do it without selling our old, used minivan and Alex's older, cheap, small commuter car. Our debt problem was not a result of us driving sports cars or car brands beyond our budget. It was all of the other expensive stuff we bought along with the trips and eating out. In addition, in our case, selling old used cars where we owed more than they were worth was not going to benefit us at all, but set us further back. So this is not an example that can help everyone.

Sell homes, boats and other high-ticket items.

We paid off our debts without selling anything major because we didn't own any items of great value. Don't think it has to be done by selling something. In some cases, however, it might be a very wise idea, especially if the item you are selling was a contributor to your debt!

Again, it's not a popular tip, but these might be a little easier to part with as they are not necessary to live life. Most everyone needs a reliable form of transportation to get to their jobs and to carry on with their lives, but rarely does anyone need an expensive home, boat or recreational vehicle. We are not saying you have to do this. Again, we had $108,000 of debts and did not take these extremes to pay them off. These are merely ideas to speed up the process for you.

Put in all the excess monies from bonuses, inheritance, annuities or any other source of money that comes to you.

Plain and simple, put any excess money towards your debt, and you will be on the debt-free path even faster!

Debt Consolidation

Generally, we don't advise anyone to brashly obtain more debt to pay off debt. One of the credit cards we obtained a couple of years into our marriage was a credit card that sent an advertisement for a 0.00 percent interest rate for 18 months to be used as a balance transfer. Who wouldn't turn down a 0.00 percent credit card in exchange for a credit card with any interest above that? But there was a danger that ultimately led us to have yet another credit card to add to the $108,000 balance.

What was the problem? First, the new credit card did not completely pay off the old one. We transferred the $3,000 the new credit card allowed us to transfer for the 0.00 percent rate. But for us, it merely meant that we now had an extra $3,000 available on the other card. We planned to pay off the 0.00 percent balance before the 18 months. As you would suspect . . . we didn't. It went on the back burner until it was too late. In addition, only balance transfers qualified for the 0.00 percent, not new purchases, which ultimately led us further down the debt path with another creditor and several thousand more dollars of debt. Not only that, but this same 0.00 percent credit card eventually turned to a 29.99 percent interest rate due to late payments.

Now, our unsuccessful debt consolidation story does not automatically necessitate the need to state: "Don't consolidate debts!" because it can honestly be a smart plan if you actually have a plan and you actually use it to give yourself a boost in paying off your debts. It needs to be an intentional decision, not a brash one.

Chapter 9

The Secret That Changes Reality

By: Cassie

Let me share with you the secret that changes reality: mindset.

Mindset is an established set of attitudes.

Attitudes are deep-seated and hard to uproot. It usually takes an earth-shattering event—often a disaster—to cause someone to consider, to question or to change an attitude.

Your mindset is like an illusion, a magic trick. It's not necessarily reality, but it's what your mind chooses to believe. After your judgments of a situation have been solidified by that mindset, convincing you otherwise is difficult and nearly impossible.

While we were getting into our massive amount of debt, we were basing our lives on a mindset that clouded every decision we made, especially financial decisions. It was easy to justify getting into debt and even needing more debt because our mindset was telling us we were immune to money problems.

Why did our mindset make us think we were immune to money problems? Well, the classic illusion: a good, stable job. Two of them, in fact.

Alex was a software engineer for a stable company in a stable position. I was a paralegal wearing fancy suits and high heels with the perfect hair and makeup. Alex had a corner office with a view while I had a downtown, top-level window office.

We were in a good position, or so we thought. We had no reason to have money problems. We were professionals with consistent paychecks coming in every two weeks.

We could spend money on what we needed, and even better, on what we wanted. We had this under control. That's what our mindset was telling us about a young professional couple with no kids. We were immune to money problems.

But it wasn't just our perception of financial immunity that was the problem, there were several other aspects to our mindset that were an issue which so easily allowed us to justify our debt.

We thought we deserved these things because we were working hard in our jobs and because we had worked hard in school and life to get to this point. The life we wanted was the promised reward for going to school and getting good jobs.

We thought we could pay it off in the near future with these amazing jobs.

We thought waiting was not the American thing to do.

We thought debt wouldn't hurt anything.

Our mindset also told us that if the banks and financial institutions were approving us for loans, then we must be able to afford it. We didn't give a second thought to the reality of our daily habits and expenses. We never even considered the foolishness of getting into debt and the actual cost the debts would bring through our lifetime.

So here we were, mindlessly diving deeper and deeper into debt to the final tune of over $108,000 in consumer debt. It would take time to change that mindset and a huge wake up call. For us, it was that earth-shattering event of discovering we were going to be parents and having no way to pay our current bills, let alone care for a new child. It took us finding, naming and owning that "why" that we talked about earlier to finally see through the financial illusion we were living under and basing our lives on. But it wasn't easy.

Mindset not only controls your own lifestyle, decisions and habits, it also controls how you perceive the world around you. Even after everything I just shared about mindset, I still to this day have a preconceived notion about the lives other people live when the reality of their situation is often very different than what I am thinking.

A Muddled Mindset

Let me share an example of a preconceived notion from one of my grocery shopping trips. The situation that transpired completely knocked my mindset off kilter. Although it was several years ago, it continuously comes to mind because it left such an impact as it revealed to me that the illusion I had in my mind was just false.

I had to go shopping with my baby, a toddler and a couple of kids. There are not many things more humbling than taking tired, cranky babies, toddlers and children to the grocery store. It's like a stage show of all of your parenting deficiencies in a 30-minute shopping trip. At least that's how I often feel when I shop with kids.

I was on the verge of pulling my hair out. I felt so frazzled and irritated, and I thought about how miserable I was at that moment.

I went to the checkout, and the gal in front of me awed me. She was wearing a nice, fancy, designer suit, high heels, perfect hair and perfect makeup. She had a warm smile, great attitude and exuded confidence with every move she made. As we were waiting in line, I was feeling so down on myself.

There I was, with a fussy baby, a curious toddler and whiny kids. I had on my frumpy "who knows exactly how old" t-shirt and a pair of eight-year-old jeans. I hadn't showered that day, but just applied deodorant on top of yesterday's scents, wiped the running mascara from under my eyes and had put my hair in a messy bun . . . not an intentional kind, but the "I've got 30 seconds to do my hair before the next kid interrupts with their so-called emergencies" type of messy bun. I noticed my unkempt children at the moment. I try to fix them up before leaving, but I realized my daughter's hair was still messy and my son had a little bit of breakfast still on his face. Not to mention my other child looked like he had used his shirt as a napkin.

To make matters worse, I had my coupon binder open and a pile of coupons in one hand and my list in the other, juggling all of this trying to keep the baby from dumping my coupons and the toddler from touching everything in sight, all the while getting my cash ready. It was like I was screaming at the top of my lungs, "Yes, I am pinching every penny possible."

I was so embarrassed to be the frumpy, frugal, frazzled freak standing there with this gal that had the seemingly perfect life.

As we were in line, I just started imagining what her life was like, what kind of corporate, high-paying job she had, what kind of adventures she could take, what kind of car she drove, the shopping trips she could take for clothes and shoes as opposed to the fruit snacks and mac and cheese crowning my very full cart. I had dreamed up this perfect life for this gal. Her face and her dress said it all: life was just too perfect for her.

Despite how I felt in those moments, my kids bumped into her and she was kind and warm and very understanding as I was profusely apologizing, worried that a kid had left a stain on her suit. But I felt like she was saying, "Wow, I am glad I am not in that desperate situation, with four kids, using coupons, all while being barely put together." Yes, my mindset went from one extreme to the other.

It was her turn to checkout. She had only four items: a gift bag, a birthday card, tissue paper and a pack of gum.

The cashier rang the items up and stated, "That will be $13.43."

The gal so elegantly pulled out her card from her designer purse and handed it to the cashier with a warm smile. I hung my head feeling so low.

A moment later, the cashier said, "This card isn't going through."

The gal responded, "Can you try again?"

Over the course of the next few minutes, three cards were swiped, her confidence quickly fading into utter anxiety as each new swipe attempt occurred.

To my disbelief, the third card was also rejected. I may have let out a gasp, but I hope it was only in my mind.

The cashier said, "What would you like to do?"

What was she going to do? Sweep floors? Wash windows? What? Instead, the gal flung open another part of her purse.

The gal very quietly leaned into the cashier and said, "Could you take the gum off?" The gum was taken off. The balance was $11.67.

She rummaged through her wallet for what seemed like an eternity. It was getting more uncomfortable for me to pretend to not notice anything was wrong.

She handed over some dollar bills and a handful of change. She was $0.20 short after all of that rummaging.

I wanted so badly to just pay for her order and end her misery, but I also knew by her sudden onset of the cold shoulder that this would have been far more degrading for her if, I, the barely put-together mom of four with my shopping list and coupon binder, paid for her order.

She didn't look at me at all the rest of the checkout, and I pretended to be oblivious to her situation by my four convenient distractions. The cashier must have gained a sudden urge of affinity as she nodded her head and said, "I'll take care of the balance."

This gal didn't even mutter a quick thanks (or at least I can't remember it to this day), quickly grabbed her items and hightailed out of that store so fast that she could have won the Olympics speed-walking competition in high heels.

After that incredibly painful few minutes, my mindset changed.

Here I was thinking so low of myself based on unsubstantiated facts, outward appearances or illusions. But I was standing there debt free, a cart bursting at the seams with groceries with no concern of how I was going to pay for them.

Even though this shopping trip was several years ago, the situation sticks out in my mind like a sore thumb to this day because it really shook my mindset to the core.

And that is because this gal was me. This gal was me 10 years earlier.

More Money, More Problems

There we were back then, a young couple with no kids and both with great jobs and quite decent pay. We were DINKs . . . *Double Income, No Kids*.

When you think of DINKs, you think more money, no problems.

But remember, that mindset got us into over $100,000 of consumer debt.

What does $108,000 of consumer debt look like?

It looks like taking vacations we couldn't afford.

It looks like buying diamonds and jewelry I didn't need.

It looks like furnishing an apartment so that no one thought we couldn't handle this "adult thing" if we didn't have an apartment full of new furniture.

It looks like buying the cars we thought we should be driving to work to look like professionals.

It looks like eating at restaurants that we couldn't afford.

It looks like trying to keep our composure while wearing our nice clothes and running a credit card for more nice clothes, only to be told by the cashier that our card was declined.

It looks like creditors and bill collectors sending the pink notices that we were 30 to 90 days overdue and we were about to have our utilities shut off.

It looks like us running to payday loans biweekly while hanging at the end of our financial rope trying to get enough cash to pay the creditor or bill collector that was screaming the loudest at the time.

It looks like receiving legal notices in the mail stating our account had been sent to the collections agency for being 120 days overdue.

It looks like having your credit pulled in one last attempt to get another loan only to be rejected and not receive even a penny.

It looks like being a paycheck away from bankruptcy.

It looks like finally waking up one day to find your "why" to say . . . NO MORE and begin working hard to get out of it.

Changing Your Mindset

Life is not always what we perceive. We cannot make decisions based on what we think might be true. We have to base our decisions on reality and choose to change our mindset to be one that reflects what is actually happening in life.

Changing your mindset is not magical. It is waking up and choosing to not make judgments, decisions and arrangements, big or small, based on a clouded thinking.

So now ask yourself, what is your mindset telling you? What has your mindset told you in the past about your finances and your financial situation?

Perhaps your mindset is blown away right now and you are saying, "Wow, I am glad I am not in the financial situation they were once in. Theirs is much worse."

Perhaps your mindset is saying, "I can handle debt because I have a better control of the situation, and I don't need to take the steps that this crazy couple took because my debt is not THAT BAD."

Perhaps your mindset is waking up and saying, "I am heading down a dangerous financial path, and it's time to get out, find my why and be motivated to change."

Perhaps your mindset is saying, "I am debt free now and I choose to remain debt-free, because of the internal damage, whether unseen or unspoken, that debt creates, no matter what that looks like to the outside world."

Perhaps your mindset is saying, "You know what, I am headed down this same path this couple was in, and I can't think of myself as being immune either, and I am going to change my mindset today."

In the end, we want you to seriously consider whether there is anything in your current mindset that you need to question, to consider or even change that is causing you to live in debt.

How can you form a mindset that will lead to debt freedom, to financial freedom? To have a mindset based on reality?

We like baby steps. So changing your mindset is not going to be any different in its approach from our 2% Rule.

That's why we like to follow a process called DDDSD: Determine, Define, Decide, Shape and Drive. Yes, the five steps are necessary for a successful venture into changing your mindset about something. When it comes to your finances, something so personal, so intimate and the driving force behind your lifestyle that you have created for yourself, it's absolutely necessary.

1. Determine

The first step in changing your mindset is to take a mental evaluation and determine what factors in your life have caused you to develop your current mindset. In fact, we recommend not just taking mental notes, but actually writing down the results of your mental evaluation. When things are written down in front of you, you can see them much more clearly and directly.

Start by asking these questions:

- What have been the major influences in your life?
- Who have been the major influencers in your life?
- What are your life experiences?
- What trials have you experienced?
- What cultural influences have you experienced?
- What influences do peer groups and other people exert on you?
- What are your family influences?
- What are your religious influences?

The next step is to determine which of these influences have been positive or negative.

For us, we had many positive and negative influences that greatly influenced our financial lifestyle.

We looked at our older co-workers and saw the lifestyles they lived. We saw our own parents and the lifestyles they had at the time we were adults. But we were forgetting they had to start somewhere. We were probably too little to notice our parents' struggles and sacrifices in the first years of our lives. By the time we were older, we were inattentive to the responsible handling of money as we were wrapped up in our own adolescent preoccupations.

We also saw our peers, many of whom were taking trips, buying nice homes and buying nice cars while seemingly having the "I can have it now" attitude.

We were influenced by our culture and what is expected and the world's definition of success, with television and movies being a prime influence.

All of this was before social media became a factor. We imagine that it is at least twice as hard today to not allow those influences to creep up and settle in.

2. Define

Using the information that you gathered in Step 1, it's now time for you to define what you want your mindset to be, and using the experiences from the positive and negative influences above, make a financially sound, responsible, solid mindset regarding money, debt and finances.

For us, one of the most positive influences regarding finances were those around us who maintained healthy money habits. We wanted this to form our basis. Looking at the influencers in our own lives and the lives of those around us in the category of good financial responsibility were those that followed many wise ideas behind finances, displaying responsibility, charitable hearts, patience and a fair of amount of debt-free living. These were the characteristics we wanted to model ourselves.

3. Decide

Now, with the information you have defined in Step 2, you need to make an intentional decision about what you want your mindset to tell you. You have to make this deliberate and intentional distinction and direction in your life. You can't just wake up one day and let the cookies crumble how they may. No, you need to decide today and DAILY what your day, week, month, year and life will hold and how you plan to get there.

Mentioning that our definition of what we wanted our financial mindset to be regarding those influencers mentioned above, we wanted to grow up to be like those that had made good financial choices.

4. Shape

Making a decision is not nearly enough. If it were, then nearly all of us would be doing something different than we are today. But our willpower is much too weak to decide and not take the all-important step of shaping and molding our mindset to stay on track with the decisions we made in Step 3.

Think about it. If we wanted to lose weight, most of us could not wake up and say "I am going to lose weight" and have the willpower to resist food temptation, have the necessary knowledge to know exactly how many calories, fat and carbs certain foods have, know exactly what type of diet we should be following for our body types or have recipes and meal plans already fully known and acted upon without research and knowledge to form a good, acceptable diet.

Even with knowledge, ideas, understanding and motivation, for most of us that is still not enough. We still make excuses like "I'm not feeling like it today," "I don't have time today" or "I didn't prep my food for today." We can easily let excuses like these affect our results that day and quickly fall off the wagon. We may jump on again for several days and off again, either reaching our goal at a painfully slow pace, not at all, or reaching the goal only to gain the weight back.

We need goals, motivators and positive influences to encourage us along the way in addition to willpower. Oftentimes, even all of that is not enough to shape us into a weight-loss mindset.

Money is no different. You will have many of the same temptations, lack of knowledge or understanding, negative influences, lack of time, lack of preparation and lack of motivation. To properly shape your mindset that you decided you needed in Step 3, you need to set a vision and goals.

Let's start with vision. You can call it your *Financial Vision Statement*. A vision statement is a statement declaring your desired end goal. It doesn't have to be long. In fact, a one-sentence vision statement is just as effective as a paragraph. It's your super long-term, lifelong goal. Make it easy to remember, make it your mantra. Create your own vision statement.

Ours is: Healthy Finances For Life

This four-word statement is the driving force of our financial lives.

The follow-up to this motivational vision statement is goal setting. Goal setting is another key to shaping your financial mindset. We know that goal setting might seem to be overrated and overused as anyone and everyone is using them so freely and lightly. But the truth is a goal is helpful.

But don't set just one goal, set many goals: big and small goals and long-term and short-term goals. Setting many goals is like a road map. In this case, it is your financial road map.

Depending on where you are in your financial journey, you may need to start with basic goals, like stop all credit card spending, pay the bills on time and actually stay in budget. That is perfectly fine and perfectly acceptable. There is no shame in defining the absolute basics. In fact, it's very commendable to remain very true to the basic necessities. Also, if you have and achieve these small goals, it means you are on track to achieve the next goals, which will get progressively larger.

5. Drive

The final step in changing your mindset is your drive. Your drive touches on two aspects—where you will steer your mindset and what you will be driving towards.

It's keeping that mindset on the path you set in Step 4.

To accomplish this, you need to remind yourself of your vision and goals regularly, perhaps daily at first. Also remind yourself, your spouse and your family about the reward at the end.

Chapter 10

THE GOLDEN TICKET
BY: CASSIE

It can be so easy to dwell on all the hard lessons we learned those first few years of our debt payoff journey that it becomes a bit more challenging to remember the little successes we experienced. Those little wins were foundational in helping us get to a point where we could see huge success later. Even more importantly, those wins gave us the tools we needed to really apply the 2% Rule.

During those first three years, there were four critical things we learned that are important to the success of a debt-free or financial plan. These were the things we did *right* during this first attempt to pay off our $108,000.

As those successes were so critical in establishing our success later on, we will share them here to help provide the foundation you'll need to get started as well.

1. An Emergency Fund Is Critical

During these first few years, one tip shared by many experts was that of setting up an emergency fund. From our own experience, this is critical.

Why?

First, you need to have a decent sum of cash on hand for a large, unexpected purchase. Medical emergencies happen. Car repairs happen. Water heaters quit working. Shingles blow off the roof. It's just a part of life.

If you don't plan for these things now, there is a very high chance that you will need to go into debt to cover them. You don't want to go into more debt, and if you keep a small crack to debt open, you may dig a deeper debt hole than the original emergency warranted.

How much should you set aside for an emergency fund?

From our own experience and in talking with others, there really is not one specific amount that will cover the needs for every family. There are too many variables. As you read our book, you will discover that we work off of percentage-based finances. Thus, the emergency fund is no different.

We recommend that each household plan to set aside about 1 to 2 percent of their gross annual income for an emergency fund. We have found 1 percent to be a bare-bones baseline that will be enough to cover most emergencies

For some families, a boost up to 2 percent of the annual household gross income may be necessary. This would especially be the case if you have an aging home, aging appliances, older cars or more people in your family.

Plan on 1 percent at the minimum and then evaluate past years' emergencies, frequency and potential upcoming issues you might already know about.

For example, if you make $50,000 a year, a 1 to 2 percent emergency fund is $500 to $1,000.

If you make $100,000 a year, $1,000 to $2,000 is your goal.

This is one of the few times that we would suggest making major sacrifices for a *very* temporary time to meet this goal. If you head to Chapter 15 you can find additional tips to help you fund your emergency fund in 30 days or less. If it takes longer, that is completely fine because you are still making progress. Don't forget this!

However, it does require sacrifice, potentially beans and rice, and hard work—all steps that are unsustainable for a prolonged period of time, but in this case only necessary for a month or so. We recommend reaching this goal quickly and then getting back on the sustainable and effective 2% Rule to meet the rest of your goals.

We also recommend setting up an emergency fund in a completely separate bank account, one that is separate from your regular bank account to make it not easily accessible.

Why do we think this is important?

1. So you don't accidentally spend it.
2. To prevent from trying to justify a weekend trip or a deserved night on the town as an emergency.
3. It needs to be saved and reserved for a real emergency.

If at any point in the process you actually need your emergency fund *for a real emergency*, once the emergency has passed, plan to refill your emergency fund so that you can be prepared for the next emergency.

2. Using Cash To Live Is Critical

Another important lesson we learned the first few years was the importance of using cash. Although this is a wise plan for any stage in your financial journey, it is critical for those working towards debt freedom.

Cash creates freedom.

It sounds counterintuitive because we often think that credit cards and a never-ending cash flow provide freedom—the freedom to spend, make last-minute decisions and do what you want.

However, the reality is that when you don't put yourself on a very clear, visual budget, you are financially insecure. You do not know what your boundaries are, or at least they are more abstract. For many, this means abstract enough to go over budget and be in bondage to debt.

Boundaries Are Important

A study done with children on a playground reveals the importance of boundaries. A group of preschool children was divided into two groups. One was taken to a playground with a fence and the other group was taken to a playground without a fence.

The hypothesis was that the children who were at the playground without a fence would exhibit more creativity, excitement, fun and freedom.

As this was put to the test, surprisingly the opposite was true.

The children in the playground without the fence huddled around the teachers and stayed close to the center of the playground. They acted in an anxious and stressed manner. Conversely, the children in the playground with the fence exhibited creative play with excitement and the freedom to explore and enjoy all the way up to the fence. In fact, they played right next to the fence.

Who knew we could learn so much from preschoolers?

The same analogy can be applied to cash-only spending. Financial freedom abounds when boundaries are clearly set.

You might think that boundaries are clearly set in the case of using a debit card. We would respond with, "*Perhaps.*" But remember, something happens to your perspective when you are physically holding the cash and physically watching the cash leave your hands. If you are in debt, we recommend using only cash for the duration of your debt-free journey. Debit cards are too abstract and far too easy to use recklessly. If you have been using cash for a while and feel that you can control spending and a debit card would be easier to manage, then by all means, use a debit card.

But, if you see yourself or a family member becoming more and more reckless with the spending, get it back in check with a cash-only system for a while.

3. Earning Additional Income Is Critical

In the midst of our initial attempt to pay off debt, we were trying as hard as we could, pulling out all the stops. We were making some progress, but at that point, it was going to take 60 years to pay off our debts because all we could afford were minimum payments. It was discouraging. It was depressing. How could it take us 4 years to get into the mess and 60 years to get out? What an unjust system!

How would we even begin to get ahead? Something had to give. Something else needed to be done. Something needed to change. But what was it? What more could we do? What more could we ask for? What other steps could we take?

How Former Presidents Of The United States Helped

It took former presidents to knock us in the side of the head and help us to find an earth-shattering answer. Seriously! Here's what these former presidents did to wake us up to the next step.

It was Presidents' Day, six weeks after our first baby was born. We were attempting to sleep in, because that's what you do when you have a day off from work, and you have a new baby. Instead we were startled awake with a big THUD on the door.

That THUD was Alex's sign to jump out of bed and grab the newspaper. We finally had a morning to read it instead of our normal practice of snatching the coupons and tossing the rest directly into the recycle bin.

Attached to the holiday newspaper like a shimmering golden ticket was the answer: WANTED: Looking for newspaper carriers immediately. Pay averages $200 per month per route.

We both saw it, both thought the same thought, and looked at each other without even needing to say a word. The answer was right in front of us on this Presidents' Day! We did need a couple of extra Lincolns and a handful of Washingtons each day to get caught up each month.

It was the perfect match. We could do this job together in the morning before work, so it wouldn't interfere with Alex's day job. It would be a good excuse to get some exercise early in the morning without a gym, and it just might be the answer we needed!

Alex filled out the application that morning. It was super fast and in 10 minutes, we had a new job that would start the next morning. We opted for two routes right next to each other, since we could drive and earn $400 per month.

The next morning, we enthusiastically jumped out of bed at 4:30. We prepared the newspapers for delivery, loaded them up into the trunk of our car, grabbed the baby and put our sleeping beauty into her car seat in the middle of the back seat. I drove and Alex sat in the back to keep an eye on baby and to jump out and deliver the newspapers.

We can't say it was easy. As we headed into the third and fourth week, waking up at 4:30 EVERY DAY without a break in the freezing cold with a new baby was tough, but we were in too much trouble to not take a paper route.

We didn't announce it to our friends or Alex's coworkers as we struggled with pride. This was a job typically known as something teenagers performed, not a married couple with a newborn and a full-time, professional job. It was easy to hide because it was too early in the morning to affect anything we were doing. We just woke up and did it.

Four hundred dollars each month was HUGE for us. It was like pure gold. When you can't even cover your bills with your current income, $400 really was like being handed a bag of gold. But we worked hard for that $400. We will not deny that! It was really hard work.

This came out to be about $13 between the two of us each day. To put this in perspective, this was $3 an hour for each of us. Although this $3 an hour was a lifesaver, there was an even greater value in this little job we had.

Greater was the lesson, insight and motivation that grew from this little job.

This little job put our debt into context. Here we were, sacrificing sleep, our pride and exerting real physical energy to make $3 per hour with the goal of paying off thousands of dollars of debt that we racked up in the blink of an eye. It was this job that helped us realize the cost of our debt. Though we may not have learned the lesson in full at that point, it was one we would refer back to time and time again to remember the pain and suffering our debt caused our family in those early years.

In the end, we didn't stay with this job for long because we soon realized we could use our extra time for jobs giving better returns on time investment.

What we needed was to increase our income. We started by delivering newspapers. Delivering newspapers might seem like an extreme side job with the demanding hours and effort, especially for the pay, but doing a job like this for a short time might help you to appreciate the money you do make on your day job and cause you to have a deeper respect for your earnings. It could also help you to consider where you distribute your funds—towards your debt or towards your diet soda—knowing the cost of hard work.

Don't worry, we are not saying this or another low-paying job is a required step and something that everyone must do. But if you're in a desperate situation where you are behind on payments, needing to get just a bit more to even meet your bills, then this type of job can be a great place to start.

Even for those that find themselves starting here, remember that this doesn't need to be long term, but is a very short-term solution to get you going on the fast track to making money on the side. The important thing to learn from our experience is that you need to start thinking outside of the box.

Don't think we ended our 2 percent income journey by delivering newspapers. This was only the start that propelled us towards understanding how critical and important that extra income can be in meeting our financial goals. Make sure to check out Chapter 14 where we show how this initial idea of delivering newspapers morphed and grew into more efficient and smarter ways to earn that extra income. We only share the newspaper delivery here as this is where we started. The huge lesson we learned was that hard work and persistence would be important in paying down our mountain of debt.

4. Cutting Your Food Budget Is Critical

Earning extra income wasn't the only positive experience we had during this difficult financial time of attempting to dump our debts fast. It was during this time that I was introduced to another approach we could use to start cutting our food budget. I was introduced to the proper method of couponing, which resulted in significant cuts to our grocery budget.

No, not the type of couponing where you spend hours clipping coupons, planning a trip, only to go to the store to find the generic products still to be much cheaper than the name-brand with the coupon. I had been through that already.

This was different. This was the secret to couponing that made it successful, and it actually worked. I was determined to use this secret approach to lower our grocery budget (see page 118).

With this newfound grocery knowledge, I could drop our weekly grocery budget to $35 a week for a family of four (two adults, a baby and a two-year-old). That was huge, that was EPIC and it was another positive step in the first three years of attempting to pay off $108,000 of consumer debts.

As a side note, today we try to live a whole-food, organic and homemade foods lifestyle while maintaining a very tight grocery budget. Couponing was a temporary tool to propel us to where we wanted to be and perhaps saved us from complete and utter financial despair at the time we needed it the most. It was a time in our lives where having this knowledge and ability to get groceries at these ridiculously low prices was what we needed to have enough money to feed our family and have just barely enough left to pay our bills. It was a stepping stone and a huge blessing.

Chapter 11

Trim It Off Slowly
Part 1: Bills
By: Cassie

Now it's time to dive into practical tips and ideas to help you find that 2 percent cut each month. Again, we want to emphasize that there is a time where you will reach your rock-bottom budget. We can't tell you when you will hit it, as every family's starting point is different.

When we started our 2 percent plan, it was actually a game, like Limbo, to see just how *low we could go* reasonably and sustainably.

Now it's time to jump into different areas of an average person's spending as we share ideas on how you can cut 2 percent. Use the next few chapters as a guide each month to help you find that decrease. Remember, the 2 percent doesn't need to all come from one category, it can be a little amount from a few categories to one cut from a single category.

We are going to share a handful of ideas in the top spending categories. We hope the information we share here gives you a springboard for several months and enough information to help you cruise through several 2 percent cuts!

Where Do I Start?

As you review your spending habits, you may see items you are paying for each month that are no longer necessary. This is a good place to start, as these are the easy cuts.

Look for items like monthly services or memberships that you are no longer using, automatic renewals and recurring fees that are not necessary, whether these are monthly or annually. Many families find these add up to a good chunk in fees that they didn't realize they were paying, You can make these 2 percent budget cuts with a simple phone call or click to cancel from your computer.

After ditching these services, memberships and fees, it is very wise to take your recurring monthly bills and look at the itemized portion to find unnecessary charges and fees.

When we did this, we were amazed at the *fees* we were paying with our monthly recurring bills that we never took the time to look at. On our cell phone bill we were paying fees for extra services that we never remember signing up for and that we weren't using, or using so infrequently, that it made no sense to pay for them. It was great that by simply looking at the itemized and detailed monthly bill statements, we could find nearly all of that month's 2 percent cut in extra, unnecessary charges that we had been paying for many months, if not years before. This resulted in success in our first month of our plan before we even cut any other expenses like our cable bill.

After you have taken the above two steps to get rid of any unnecessary services, fees and memberships, it's time to cut into each category and find some fun and creative ways to slash the budget!

Saving Tips For Utilities

It is crazy to think about how much the average person spends on this category. These expenses often seem so necessary that we mindlessly pay the bills without thinking much about how much we are really spending.

Cable

Cable TV has somehow become a necessary household expense. We are here to tell you that it is a bill that you could cut very easily. This could potentially be close to two months worth of 2 percent cuts alone!

First, cable does not remain at the promotional rate you signed up for, as that is only a temporary rate. Second, the quoted cost doesn't include the fees, box rental fees, premium channel fees, extra feature fees and other fees.

Cutting cable was one of the first things we did. Yes, we missed HGTV, Food Network and some sports, but today, we still get to watch for free on their websites and Facebook pages. Cutting cable saved us at least $500 a year—and we had only basic cable service.

We didn't go without television completely. We had an antenna we bought for $10 and were able to get about seven local channels, which carried a majority of shows we enjoyed.

We purchased a Roku device for $50 that connects us to all of the streaming options. We also have a YouTube Roku Channel, which gives us many more options for free on our television. This Roku device, along with Hulu and our annual Amazon Prime membership gives us access to thousands of television episodes and movies and saves us over $500 a year.

Worst case, if there is a show you love and it's not available for free, you can generally buy an entire season on Amazon for around $20—still a massive savings over the months you would pay for cable to get the season's worth of shows. Many video game devices and even some televisions can also act as a streaming device, so if you have one of those you probably don't even need a Roku (or other streaming device) and can save even more.

Cell phones

Let us be honest and say that saving on cell phones today is MUCH easier than it was when we started this plan. Cell phone companies have become so competitive that saving on them is easier today! So shop around to find the best deal at the time.

One of the biggest recommendations we can make is to go with a no-contract, month-to-month plan. These seem to be the best value currently, and they don't lock you into a monthly contract. When we first started, we also went to a no-contract, month-to-month plan as it saved us at least 50 percent, but the coverage was terrible because it was independently owned. Since that time, these smaller, month-to-month cell phone companies are supported by larger mother companies—thus they reap the benefits of great coverage today. So it is a smarter move.

Choose a plan where you can bring in any of your own phones. If you want to upgrade, consider buying a used or refurbished phone as a way to save big money on a smartphone.

Plans now almost always come with unlimited talk and text along with a fair amount of data that is more than enough for a family for standard data usage. Realize that increases in data usage today are for those who watch television and movies from their cell phone; this will eat up your data and cost you a lot more, even with the month-to-month plans. Ensuring your cell phone is connected via Wi-Fi when available can help reduce those data usage costs as well.

Home phones

Consider dropping the home phone entirely and just use cell phones. This will save you at least $30 a month, as a home phone is unnecessary for many in most cases. If keeping a landline for whatever reason is a priority for you, there are a couple of options to save money.

First, consider using a company that piggybacks off your Internet. Currently, these are some of the most affordable landlines available, with prices hovering around $10 a month, but watch for contract commitments and extra fees. Some cable television providers also offer this service, but don't get sucked into their offers because they are also attached to an unnecessary cable bill.

Second, bundling Internet with a landline from the same company may offer better discounts than a landline alone.

Internet

That brings us to saving on Internet. It most likely is a necessary expense, as necessary as home phones were in the 20th century. We use the Internet for everything in life these days, and with the resources at your fingertips to save money from coupons, online sales and discount offers, it is probably worth it and can nearly pay for itself when coupled with those money-saving resources.

But that doesn't mean you still can't find ways to save on this area. Just because it is probably a justifiable expense does not automatically necessitate paying a high bill.

The first thing to do is to shop around and compare prices. Once you find a deal out there that you would be happier with, consider negotiating with your current Internet provider. They don't want to lose you, and they have some leeway in the billing of your service, especially when a competitor comes into play. This alone may do wonders for your Internet bill. We've also experienced where an attempt in cancelling prompted an even better, lower permanent offer as one last attempt to keep you as their customer.

Many Internet service providers offer cable options, which are very profitable for them and they will try to upsell any cable options. Don't fall into the cable traps. You just want Internet or Internet and a landline. Adding a cable bill to save money on Internet is not going to save you money.

Consider buying your own new or refurbished modem and router as they range from about $50 to $100. This saves you the monthly rental fee of $5 to $10, which will be made up in just a few months.

Finally, consider how much speed you really need. Most households are paying for more speed than their needs require. If so, you are just wasting money. Check your speed at a site like SpeedTest.com. Why? Because if you are paying for a certain speed, but are not getting speed you were promised, you have big negotiating power, including refunds applied to your bill or prorated amounts. We have done this several times ourselves. If they promise and under-deliver, we will ask for money back.

The same goes for any downtime you had with the Internet being out. Internet service providers are willing to reimburse you for your downtime. In rare cases when a company cannot provide you their promised speeds, you might be able to cancel your contract with them as they have not fulfilled their side of the bargain. We had this happen with an Internet provider, and since we didn't receive their promised bandwidth, we were able to cancel the contract without any termination fees.

Electricity, gas and water bills

While these bills are not negotiable and you generally can't shop around, there are things you can do at home to lower these bills.

We enjoy playing a game in our home to see how low we can get our utilities. It means the whole family is challenged to shut lights off, unplug unused appliances, run the appliances during non-peak hours, take shorter showers or hang clothes to dry.

There are also other things you can do that are very beneficial like:

- Set the water heater at 120 degrees. The EPA estimates that many households lose around $60 a year by keeping standby water heated. $60 is probably about one month's worth of the 2 percent cut!

- Set the thermostat lower for heating and higher for air-conditioning. We invested in a programmable thermostat for about $25 that allowed us to program the thermostat automatically for our at-home, away and sleep times saving us money all year. Energy.gov estimates a 10 percent energy bill savings from this trick.

- Close off vents in rooms not being used, place towels or draft blockers under doors near entrances and add plastic to windows in winter to seal them off.

- To heat the house naturally, harvest the heat of southern windows in winter on sunny days by opening shades. In the summer, open windows at night and shut when daytime hits, keeping southern windows covered by drapes or shades so the cool doesn't escape as fast.

- In the winter, when you use your oven, keep it open after you are done baking to spread the heat while it cools down.

- Space heaters are a more affordable way to heat small spaces.

- Replace door sweeps and door and window draft guards. It costs less than $10 and saves great money.

- Install a low-flow faucet aerator on your faucets. They cost $2 to $3, take just a couple of minutes to install and can save water, making your faucets more water efficient. Do the same for your showerheads. It is estimated that this one switch saves most households 40 percent of the water used in their homes!

- Fix faucet leaks. Most leaks take a few simple seconds to repair and it's fixed! The average drippy faucet wastes 20 gallons of water daily—water that you are paying for.

- Convert your toilet to a low-flush toilet by creating your own water displacement system. This will save many gallons of water a day when flushing. Simply fill a few 1-liter water bottles with sand and place in the tank of your toilet. According to Rodale's Organic Life, this hack will save a half gallon of water each flush. Since the average person flushes the toilet five times a day, a family of five can save 12 to 15 flushes worth of water or about $0.12–$0.15 of water usage a day with this one-time trick.

A note on water—the national average water bill is about $0.01 per gallon of water used. If you can save 40 to 50 percent of your water usage with the tips above, you can easily find a 2 percent cut!

Savings Tips For Automobile Expenses

Obviously this one is partly set in stone. Most have to drive to work and run errands for basic necessities. However, there are ways to save on gasoline and car maintenance expenses.

Gasoline

The first consideration is how much unnecessary driving are you doing? Can you cut your trips or combine your errands? There's an app for that! Seriously! If you know the errands you need to run, do it all in one day on one slick route using free apps that plan the shortest route for you. It does wonders for saving gas money!

Here are some other tips:

- According to FuelEconomy.gov, accelerate gently, maintain a steady speed, anticipate traffic to adjust without quick reactions, avoid slamming on brakes and slow down to drive efficiently.
- Keep your tires at proper inflation for most fuel-efficient driving.
- Remove extra weight.
- Reduce idling. We often turn the car off in a drive-thru and certainly when waiting for someone.
- Keep vehicle maintained.

Auto maintenance and repairs

Now let's review the second part of car expenses—maintenance:

- Change the oil yourself! Just watch a YouTube video on how to do this. Please dispose of your oil properly by taking it to an approved oil collection center. Don't pay for oil disposal, as there are free disposal locations in your area.
- If you don't want to change the oil yourself, look for oil change coupons, coupon books or online deals for local or nationally known centers.
- Do repairs yourself. Car parts dealers can help you diagnose the problem, print off instructions and direct you to videos on how to repair your issue, while also loaning you the tools, all for free if you buy the parts through them.
- If there is something you can't do, ask around for referrals for car repairs. We have found the locally run auto repair shops seem to be the best value.
- Many tire stores will test tires and inflate for free and give even more benefits if you buy tires through them. Some of them offer free pre-roadtrip inspections.
- Sam's Club or Costco have great deals for new tires.

Insurance

Insurance is another spot in which you can save quite a bit. It's a category in which a lot of our readers have found some surprising savings after paying the same rates for several years. Giving just a bit of attention to this category might yield one to two month's worth of 2 percent cuts!

All of these ideas will apply to auto and home insurance and most will also apply to life insurance.

- Get a new quote annually. Get new quotes from other carriers and your current carrier to see if you can find a lower rate with the coverage you desire. Be sure the quotes you receive are for equal coverage as this can drastically change the rate.
- Have insurance companies compete. With your new quote, you can either switch providers or take this quote to your current provider and see if they will compete for your business. If you have been a good customer with no claims that year, it's very likely that your current insurance company will compete.
- Increase the deductible. You buy insurance to be protected in case of the unexpected. But it really is unexpected and many go their entire life without needing to make any insurance claims. We recommend increasing your deductible so that your monthly premium will be reduced. Remember to consider your deductible amount when setting up your emergency fund.
- Get the minimum coverage needed on your vehicle. If you own your vehicle, one way to save is to only carry liability coverage on your car. You typically are only required to get comprehensive if you still owe your lender money on your vehicle. Do talk to your insurance agent to see what other coverage options they would recommend, such as uninsured driver and medical expenses.
- Ask about any of the following discounts with a new or current carrier:
  - Discounts for having safety measures in place like alarm systems—The most common is an alarm or security system.
  - Discounts for professionals—This one was new to us a couple of years ago when we evaluated our policy and discovered that we could receive an additional discount for being a professional.
  - Discounts for marital status—If you are married, you may get additional discounts.
  - Good credit discounts—If you have decent or good credit, this may also give you an additional discount!
  - Good driver discounts—If you are typically a good driver with no violations on your record, you can get a discount. You will want to check with your state as to how long violations will stay on your record. It varies from state to state and from violation to violation, but the average for minor traffic violations is two years.

- Good student discounts—Much like credit rating for adults, a student's good grades are often used to judge the responsibility factor of a teen, so if you have a good student in your house, you may earn some extra discounts.
- Low mileage discount—If you do not drive a lot, usually less than 8,000 miles per year, you may be eligible for additional discounts.
- Only insure rebuilding costs, not the cost of the land. If the unexpected were to happen, it is most likely going to happen to your home and the claim you would be making would be the cost to rebuild your home—not the land! The land your home sits on is generally included in the total value of your home, but you will be able to reuse the land, so there is no sense in insuring the land.
- Pay your policy in a six month or one year lump sum. This is another common discount among insurance providers. Many will give you a dollar amount discount or percentage off discount by paying your premiums for a full six months or even one year.
- Check with your employer to see if they have a group discount for homeowners, life or auto insurance. Many companies have a group purchasing discount—you can think of it like a co-op. Some larger companies will offer this discount as an added fringe benefit by allowing employees to buy into the group plan.
- Combine policies with one company. Another common discount is the multiple policy discount. Many insurance providers will give you discounts if you also purchase your car insurance or life insurance with your homeowner's policy.

Christmas Or Holidays Gifts

Christmas can be expensive if you get caught up in using credit to celebrate. In fact, in a survey of recent Christmas spending, the average household obtained $986 in debt for Christmas. When asked, 73 percent of the consumers surveyed planned to pay it all off in one to six months, but 27 percent said they plan to only pay the minimum payment. If they obtained the debt at the average of 14 percent interest rate, it would take 104 months to pay it off at the minimum.

That means that one out of four consumers may still be paying for that Christmas eight years later.

The 73 percent who plan to pay it off within six months are still paying for the past Christmas, probably even before starting a savings for the upcoming Christmas.

No matter what debts you are paying today, whether last year's Christmas or Christmas from eight years ago, start saving TODAY for this upcoming Christmas. Start a separate savings account that you don't touch except for your Christmas shopping so you have a debt-free Christmas. And yes, you are going to start saving for the coming Christmas before past ones are paid off. In fact, you are going to start saving for Christmas before your debts paid off.

It might already be obvious why, but the reality of it is that Christmas happens every year whether you want it to or not. I can tell you that your kids are not going to be happy if you skip Christmas. It will not work, as you could already guess.

But, if you don't break the Christmas debt cycle now, it will keep going year after year.

How Much Should You Save For Christmas?

Financial advisors all across the board recommend saving 1 percent of your gross income for Christmas. So when your paycheck comes, before determining how much you can devote to your debts or other financial goals, take 1 percent out of the gross check and put it in a savings account. If you make $36,000 a year, you should have saved $360. If you make $75,000, you should have saved $750, and so on.

If you wish to spend more than this, that's fine. But, if you are in debt, we recommend working outside of the 2% Rule to achieve this goal. We don't want you working the 2% Rule just to pay for Christmas. The 2 percent spending decrease and 2 percent income increase should be earmarked for your current debts and financial goals.

So with the 2% Rule, if you need to cut $60 and make $60 to meet this month's goal, but you want to put an *extra* $600 in your Christmas fund, you need to find or make an extra $50 a month outside of your month's goal.

If you do have only $360 to spend on Christmas, don't think of it in terms of retail prices because that $360 will not go far. But nearly everything we buy for Christmas has been 50, 60, even 70 percent off with the great sales, stacking coupons and buying things with discounted gift cards. If I have $360 to spend, and I get everything for at least 50 percent off, it's as if I really had $720 to spend!

When we started this plan, we did save 1 percent for Christmas, and it was a HUGE blessing!! But what was even more fun was creatively spending the money. In those first years, we were able to spend much less.

We discovered that kids don't need everything as brand new. We bought some *very* nice things for our children that were gently used. The kids had no idea, and we saved loads of money!

One Christmas we had two little girls who wanted a play kitchen. Someone in the classifieds was selling a play kitchen for $10 within a mile of our house. We looked at this kitchen, and it was in nearly perfect condition, it just needed a good wipe down.

We purchased this kitchen for $10 along with two big boxes of accessories for an additional $20. So they got a play kitchen and tons of accessories for $30!

Five years later, we sold this play kitchen in our own garage sale for $5.

Second-hand purchases can save so much money, especially for toys and name-brand clothing.

Also, I am very particular about how I use those 40 to 50 percent off craft store coupons. These are very valuable coupons. For example, my mom is organized and loves to plan. I found a beautiful planner at the craft store for $12, and I had a 40 percent off coupon. Combined with some homemade bath salts, candles and more, I had a nice gift that was perfect for her!

Don't forget those fantastic $10 off a $10 purchase or $10 off a $25 purchase coupons from department stores! Hit the clothing clearances and find an item right over $10 and get it practically for free!

Plan your Christmas shopping early in the year and build up your inventory. For example, T-shirts are perfect for many men, no matter the season. If I buy a T-shirt in June on sale for $10 and use the $10 off $10 purchase coupon, I really get it for free. That free T-shirt is a perfect gift come December.

I also start shopping for Christmas at the after-Christmas sales the previous year. I buy those beautiful scarf, glove and hat sets for 90 percent off and save them for 11 months.

Since we always save 1 percent of our gross income per paycheck for Christmas, we have money year-round in the Christmas fund to start shopping even right after Christmas. So all year, I am on the lookout for possible great gifts for anyone on our list and am able to save a bundle!

We generally start toy shopping around August then shop through October. Why? Well, these times have the best toy clearance prices. The stores are clearing out last year's toys to make room for all the brand new inventory that will begin arriving the end of October.

Another way to spend less for Christmas is to make the gifts you give. Homemade gifts are so sweet and kind for family and friends. They often mean much more than store-bought gifts. We have also made gift baskets from our supply of coupon deals like bath items, specialty foods, etc.

I love essential oils. I can take one $15 bottle of essential oil that has approximately 300 drops and make dozens of beautiful mesh baggies or bottles of bath salts, fizzy bath bombs, sugar scrubs and more for a pampering gift basket. The gift receiver loves these special treats that they wouldn't normally make or buy for themselves.

If you can't tell, Christmas shopping is my favorite! I have a designated budget, we don't go into debt and I love to play the game of how much can I get for my 1 percent each year! It's one of my most pleasurable spending categories for the year without stress and without debt!

I challenge you to have an enjoyable, fun, Christmas shopping year!

That leads me into birthdays and other events. Because I am grabbing these deals all year, we have a full gift bin to be able to give nice gifts on a budget! All of these findings go into a gift bin and when the kids have a birthday party or other event where a gift is needed, we shop from home.

Occasionally, we do need to buy a gift we don't have. Places like bookstores and craft stores have crazy, good coupons all year, like 30 to 50 percent off one item. Find an item that fits in the budget and see how much you can get.

Chapter 12

TRIM IT OFF SLOWLY PART 2: LIVING EXPENSES

BY: CASSIE

We identify living expenses as the expenses that you have when the need arises. They are not necessary monthly recurring expenses, but they are still a vital part of living as they include food and clothes.

We, along with many of our readers, have found this area to be one of the most fun categories to creatively drop our expenses in each and every month.

Why?

Well, there is quite a bit of wiggle room in these categories for most families. It's fun to play that 2 percent Limbo game of *how low can you go?*

As mentioned previously, we are merely going to scratch the surface in each of these categories to help give you a jumping off point to drop each area, but there are so many savings ideas that we could have a whole book dedicated to them! But these ideas shared here will be enough to get you started and going for many months into your journey!

Savings Tips For Clothing

This is an area where you can save big time! I love to shop for clothes, shoes and accessories, and I spent a lot of money doing so in the past! Today, I spend very little. VERY little. For new clothing, it's not uncommon for me to go to a department store and spend $150 and save $1,500. I can do this two or three times a year when all of their "sale stars" align. I can combine last season's 80 percent off clearances with money off coupons, percent off coupons and earn store cash in return.

And no, I am NOT getting store credit card discounts. I can't buy used clothes this cheap. It does only happen a couple of times a year, and my stack of cash I've been saving from those prior months is ready. For a family of eight, I can refill wardrobes where needed, shopping with the lump sum of cash saved from the many previous months.

I have also found similar deals at kids clothing stores. I recently got all three boys' current summer wear and upcoming winter clothes for $80 (35 pieces of clothing, an $800 value).

I plan for these sales throughout the year by contributing to my allotted clothing budget each month so there is a nice stack of cash in there when it is needed. I can tell you; it is one of the most fun shopping experiences ever and definitely worth the wait.

I couldn't save like this out of the gate! It was a few years into our financial journey before I learned about and planned for these sales, and it just continuously gets better the more I learn.

Here are some of those ideas to cut back on clothing expenses:

- Start a clothing rotation with your circle of friends, family, church, neighbors, moms' groups.
- Buy secondhand; preferably at garage sales as you have negotiating power and generally much lower prices than a thrift store. Thrift stores are great for teens and kids wanting name brand labels, especially when combined with discounts and coupons. Whenever you visit a thrift store, donate something and request a coupon for a percentage off your total order.
- Save clothes for future kids. We store seasonal bins in our basement and keep a handful of clothes for each kid's upcoming size and season so I have clothes on hand just in case.
- Ask for clothes. If you just ask friends and family for any clothes they are not using, you will get an amazing response. I have done this, and we have received many more items than we could use nearly every time.
- Shop out of season. Buy now, and enjoy that brand new clothing in nine months. I love it when the clearances are 75 percent off or more.
- Fix your current clothes. With a little mending and stitching know-how, you can mend and re-wear current clothes.
- Stick with basics for everyone. I wear the same shirts in the winter as I do the summer by just layering. It keeps my wardrobe simple, and then I only need a few outer layer pieces to add in the winter or fall.

Savings Tips For Eating Out

Eating out is one of our family's joys and pleasures. It's one of the reasons we got into so much debt early in our marriage. We still enjoy eating out, and that is why we love the 2% Rule. We can still enjoy going to restaurants by becoming more creative with how we do it.

In the other get out of debt plans we tried, eating out was a no-go. These plans said to sacrifice eating out to pay off your debts. This was one of the pitfalls for us. We have learned we can enjoy eating out with a creative approach and stay within a rock-bottom budget.

Where we eat out is determined by the many factors listed below. It also means that we get to enjoy different restaurants based on discounts and promotions offered at the time.

Here are some eating out tips:

- Eat by paying for your bill with gift cards gifted to you or by purchasing gift cards beforehand at a discount. We buy discounted gift cards for 5 to 20 percent off through gift card buying and reselling sites. I've also earned free gift cards with surveys and online tasks.
- Combine those gift cards with in-restaurant coupons. Those coupons and promotions can be combined with your discount gift card since the gift card acts as cash.
- Join restaurant email lists for free food, often a free drink, appetizer or dessert. We often use the free appetizer as a meal for one or two of our younger children. Sign up at least 24 hours before you want to visit that establishment, as most restaurants will not send the promotion out immediately.
- Look for specific promotions like a free birthday meal or dessert, kids eat free or buy-one get-one-free promotions. Again, you can combine your discounted gift cards with these promotions.
- In addition to all the tips above, we also believe in creative ordering to save money. Here are some real life examples of how we have creatively ordered:
  - We rarely order drinks. Drinks are often 25 to 30 percent of the entree prices. When it is just the two of us, it's a huge savings! When it is all eight of us, that's an even larger savings! We can enjoy those same drinks at home for pennies on the restaurant dollar.
  - We also rarely have dessert, unless we have a free coupon or a birthday treat, and then we all share.
  - We enjoy late lunches or early dinners, like the two or three o'clock hour. We pay lunch prices, and then we just have a light snack for dinner.
  - We've found that it is often much cheaper to have two to three younger kids split one adult entree rather than ordering two or three kid's meals.
  - We help our kids order food that is actually filling and a good value (not the mac and cheese for $3.99).
- We like to eat at restaurants that have affordable bottomless appetizers or sides or pre-meal eats. Most major chain restaurants have this from chips, fries or breads. It helps fill kids a little more, making splitting entrees a more viable option.
- We always add on the side salad for $0.99 if all of us are eating. We adults will share one salad and the kids share the other add-on salad from the second adult entree.

- We order large. What we mean is that one of our favorite pasta restaurants has a dish that is normal size. For only a couple of dollars more, we can upgrade to large size, which nearly doubles the portions. It makes for a cheap lunch the next day when paired with sides. This is the same for the occasional steak dinners. We upgrade to the larger size, eat half in the restaurant and take half home. The leftovers become a second meal in some way when it only costs a few dollars more.

- Alex and I will often split one entree when eating out too. Many restaurant entrees are much larger than we can eat in one sitting. But splitting saves us money and calories. We also add on the salad to expand the entree.

A Latte Of Coffee

Another real-life example of cost savings is happening as we are sitting in a local coffee shop with free Wi-Fi to write this book. Yes, the coffee shop was our book-writing home. Try writing a book with six kids 13 and under running around at home. We would be type-mumbling through this book. While our friend watches our kids a couple of days a week for several weeks—we've written a book!

We laugh because as we are writing this section, we are sitting here sipping our coffee and tea using the tips we share above. Our Costco sells $50 worth of gift cards to this local coffee shop chain for $39.99 (getting our 2 percent Costco reward too). Then, while in the coffee shop, we signed up for their rewards program, which gives us 15 percent back in coffee cash. Once it hits a certain amount, we get that money off our next bill. So it seems like every third or fourth visit, we get free coffee! Double-stacked savings, free Wi-Fi, mumble-free writing. Win-win for all.

In the end, we save at least 50 percent every time we eat out, but many times, it's more like 60 to 70 percent when we combine a buy one get one free promotion with our discount gift cards and use creative ordering.

We do want to make one note here regarding tipping. Please don't cheapen your tip. We always tip the full amount before discounts. There have been many times that our tip has exceeded our actual out-of-pocket bill. Even though we are saving a huge amount of money on the food, the service is not discounted. These men and women work hard too, so we always base our tipping on the full price. It's a cost we factor in before eating out.

Savings Tips For Dates And Entertainment

When it comes to spending time together, we enjoy many activities and events. We used to spend a decent amount of money monthly in this category. We just thought money was to be spent. This is not a totally free section for us, but we look for big discounts if we do have to pay anything.

Once you know how much you have spent in the past on this category, you may realize it is more than you thought, and you may have some room to find those 2 percent cuts.

I know some families that already only do the free things and events. That's great! If you are already pretty much spending free time together as a couple or as a family, then continue doing so!

Here's how to save on dates and entertainment:

- For movies, if you can't wait for "date night in" at home with a free or cheap rental on a movie, consider going to the movie when it hits the cheap theater in your area. If we wait a month or so, our entire family of eight can attend the movies and get popcorn for less than $30. When it is just the two of us, it's less than $10.
- If you must go to a first run movie—even in our debt-payoff days, we HAD to see Lord of the Rings movies on the first run—go to the matinee. Buy your tickets from the theater directly beforehand instead of online to avoid fees. Look for discounted gift cards for the specific movie theater through buy/sell gift card sites.
- Pick a local attraction that offers reciprocal discounts to other attractions. In other words, buy a membership that will also give you free (or deeply discounted) admission to other spots in your local area. For example, my kids love a certain museum in our area, but the annual membership is expensive. I found that if I bought a cheaper annual membership to a local animal park, not only did I save money there, but because this museum was listed as a reciprocating attraction, we could get in free to that museum, and we were able to save a lot of money. This will require a bit of research and the attractions are subject to change at any time, but visiting the websites will tell you the prices and the reciprocating attractions
- Sign-up for email lists to museums, parks and other attractions. Very often, you will receive discount days, coupons or promotions.
- Follow your favorite spots online to hear about special discounts as well.
- Ask if there is a discount! There is a local theme park in our area that our family wanted to visit badly. I wanted to find discounts to stay within our entertainment budget. I couldn't find any for the day we had available. I called the park and talked with customer service. I received some insider hints on where to find some nice discounts for that day! It NEVER hurts to ask!
- If you are a military family, you will almost always find a discount to local attractions.

- Visit on the free days. Nearly every zoo, museum and aquarium in our area has free days. Just follow them on social media and sign up for their emails. Plan to go on those days, but be prepared for an onslaught of people!
- Don't forget local parks and other free attractions. A walk in the park for a romantic date night or a park play date with the kids doesn't cost a thing. Plus, pack a picnic! My kids LOVE to eat at the park. They would choose this most any day over any paid attraction.
- Libraries are also great spots that offer activities including reading times, craft times and other fun events.
- Follow your city or county social media accounts to watch for free concerts, carnivals and events in your local community. You will likely find more to do than you have time for.
- Use the group buying coupon sites. My kids enjoy the trampoline park here and this is how we go.
- Where allowed, take your own snacks, food and water. We often find that the food at these places is highly overpriced.
- Stack your savings with discount gift cards. Costco sells discount gift cards for national attractions but also for local attractions. For our son's tenth birthday, he wanted to visit a local mini-theme park. An unlimited daily pass for all attractions was $25. Well, it is free for the birthday child on their birthday, so we registered his birthday to receive a free pass for him. For his siblings, we bought $100 worth of gift cards at Costco for $75. On the park website, they offered $5 off coupons for the unlimited passes. In the end, my out-of-pocket expense was $75, which covered our five kids enjoying all the activities for an unlimited amount of time, and we saved $50. This was all just from being smart about stacking savings.
- Use coupons combined with discount gift cards whenever you find them. No matter what, you should at least be able to find a coupon. A quick Internet search will usually produce coupon results.

In the end, you might find quite a few months' worth of 2 percent cuts just in this category. As you settle into a monthly budget amount you can get more creative with how you spend your entertainment budget each month. I love to see how much we can do for the rock-bottom amount budgeted.

Savings Tips For Salon Services

I can tell you right now that salon services were also one of the first things to go in the early months of our 2% Rule. This is another area, depending on how much you spend now, where you could see several months of 2 percent savings.

To save in the area of haircuts, other hair services and other salon services, we basically do two main things.

First, I learned how to cut boys' hair. I bought a $20 haircutting kit online and watched the provided video and practiced on my little boys. Then I started cutting Alex's hair at home too. We have done this now for years. None of our boys have ever had their hair cut by someone other than me. We save at least $10 to $15 a month just on Alex.

I also cut my girls' bangs. It's easy and saves me $10 each bang trim over a salon.

Now we have three daughters with gorgeous long hair. Cutting their beautiful hair scares me. So we have a salon alternative that I have personally been going to for the past 13 years: the beauty college.

The prices are CRAZY low and they use top-of-the-line beauty products. Yes, your hair and salon services are being done by a student, but you can ask for a senior student if you are concerned. In 13 years, my girls and I have never walked out with a bad cut because once your hair is done, one of the teachers inspects and cleans it up if needed. There really isn't a lot a student can do to mess it up so badly that a teacher cannot fix.

Now, I am a low-maintenance type of gal, but even with that, I have also received colors, tints or highlights from the beauty college and it is beautiful every time for a fraction of the cost. We don't go to the salon monthly, but we budget $10 per month because we go about every three months and spend about $30. Cuts are $5, and this leaves room for a specialty service and tip.

This is also a good place to go for other salon services like pedicures, nails, manicures, cosmetic services or waxing. Thankfully, I have three very eager girls that beg to do my nails, so I am set.

Savings Tips For Travel

We love traveling. If you have read our book up to this point, you already know that travel was a great source of financial and debt stress.

The Traveling Life

I grew up traveling all of the time. I saw so much of the country and created amazing memories.

So when I left home, I wanted that same traveling lifestyle, even though I didn't grow up in a wealthy house. I grew up in quite a frugal house, but I didn't see the frugality. I saw what my parents were able to do for us, and I wanted to take that with me when I left home.

My parents were able to do all of this traveling because it was part of my dad's job. He was required to travel for work for about half of the time. We just had the side benefit of being able to go on business trips with him, and my parents could do it because we didn't have the extra hotel room expenses. His company paid for his hotel room, whether it was just him or the five of us.

He also got a per diem for food, which meant that my mom planned our food to be able to feed the whole family for the cost of just his per diem. His flight would be reimbursed, but if we all went, he was reimbursed the value of the ticket that my parents turned into gas money for a road trip. My family did not have a lot of money. They were just creative with what they had!

Unfortunately, I wasn't paying enough attention to notice how they were able to take us all over the country. I just liked the fact that I went all over the country, and I wanted to take my husband and one day, my kids, all over too. However, as you have read our story, you will know that this is one of the areas that pushed us further into debt.

Today, we still travel, but now we plan, research, save and are creative in how we do it. The BIGGEST factor is to save. If you have the money saved, whether you chose to have a scrimp-and-save trip or a no-money-worries trip, you need to plan accordingly. Saving for your trip before you go will save you from putting it on your credit card.

Beyond saving beforehand, there are numerous travel savings tips and so many available discount travel sites. We will walk you through the steps we take to plan and save for a trip.

Hotel

- Find prices on a hotel comparison site to get a good basis for a price range.
- Find a few hotels that fit within the nightly budget you are willing to spend, then head to these hotels' specific sites and compare rates. Often, the prices are better than most travel sites.
- Join the hotels' email newsletters and rewards clubs. These sometimes automatically generate a deal.
- Check club and membership deals like AAA, military, insurance, cell phone company or coupon books.
- Call the local hotel location directly. If you can talk to an actual person at the actual physical hotel, not the national reservation line, you can generally beat any of the online prices they offer.
- Check group buying sites.
- If you have a reservation, keep checking rates once you have a final booking. If you find a lower rate on that same hotel, call them and they will most likely match that rate.
- Personally call and ask for the rates you've received on previous trips. This works most of the time, except during an exceptionally busy season.

Rental car

We actually follow the same process detailed above for hotels when we reserve a car. It works the same way!

At the time of rental, here are some recommendations:

- When you pick up your car, ask for a free upgrade. They have no obligation to do so, but if you are nice to the agent they will sometimes upgrade you for free or for a deeply discounted price.
- Inspect the car thoroughly. Find every flaw, scratch, dent, imperfection with the car. Most are fine with minor wear and tear on the vehicle, but you never want to leave the rental car lot with a question of whether you will be responsible for an imperfection, either major or minor.
- Never get any of the extras. Double-check beforehand, but your car insurance likely covers rental cars. If so, you don't need the rental company's insurance. Be aware however, you may still be responsible for the daily fee of the downtime the car is out of service while being repaired. The same ideas apply to roadside assistance. If you have insurance or a car club type membership, these generally cover you. Don't pay for navigation systems if your phones have navigation.
- Choose only one driver. If you have more than one driver, you will pay double or more for your rental. Unless you really need two drivers, just choose one person to drive the whole time. Some rental car companies will allow a spouse to drive for free.
- Take your own infant car seats (airlines do not charge for them). Car seats may cost more than the cost of the rental.
- Opt to pay for your own gas and fill the vehicle up before dropping it off.

Airline tickets

This one is a bit trickier. Once you book your flight, that's your rate. There are times you might get a refund for a lower rate, but it's difficult and often comes with a fee.

That's why we prefer to shop at the known *low ticket price times* and use a site that can help predict whether the rates will drop and buy when they suggest. We have found that these airfare predictions are fairly accurate.

Here's the process we go through:

- Start at travel sites that compare many airlines and rates.
- Once you've gotten an idea of who will be the lowest, search that company's site directly.
- Start an airfare rate prediction request with a site that will inform you when rates drop.
- The lowest published prices are generally offered late evening or early morning on a Tuesday or Wednesday. The same goes for tickets purchased with airline miles. Your airline mile rate will often change with the price changes.
- Purchase when the airfare rate prediction site tells you to.
- You can always ask for an upgrade. It never hurts to ask, but don't count on it.

- If you are willing to be bumped you can make a pretty penny!
- Always sign up for airline miles, and always claim them each flight.

Spartan Alex

Starting in 2015, Alex went on a personal quest to lose weight and get healthy. He had just turned 40 and wanted to be a new person in his mid-life. Well, he actually applied the 2% Rule for his health, weight and exercise. He successfully lost nearly 100 pounds. He started running in January, ran his first 5K that July and continued to run races to help motivate himself. Then he ran an OCR Race. What is an OCR race? Basically, it's Obstacle Course Racing—running various distances combined with a couple of dozen obstacles. He fell in love and wanted to beat records and push himself. So for his birthday and for Christmas in 2015, our family gave him an annual pass for the 2016 OCR races. This meant that he could run an unlimited number of races for the whole year. It's a super deal if you run more than three races a year.

He ran 11 OCR races with his annual pass. A few races were local or within a few hours drive, but many were not. In his year of OCR racing his travels cost less than $150 each trip that required an overnight stay and a flight.

How did we do it?

- We used a Christian hospitality network for a free place to stay for most trips. One trip he split the cost of a cheap, basic hotel room with a buddy that was running and for another trip the whole family went and made a family vacation out of it.
- He flew with his accumulated airline miles. He used the airfare tips above to get the best value for his airline miles, spending the least amount per flight. So he flew to every destination for the $11 in fees.
- For some of the trips, he needed an overnight rental car. He usually paid less than $20 plus taxes and fees.
- He took his own cereal, granola bars and non-perishable food. Once he landed, he would grab some fresh food for around $20.

He had a wonderful year and in the end the 11 races cost less than $1,000 total. See what debt freedom can do? Even though we had the freedom for him to have this fun year of OCR racing, we still planned and scrimped so he could do more with the budget we set aside for his adventures!

Savings Tips For Large Purchases

The first tip we want to share in this area is to consider using the overnight rule as shared by Rachel Cruz regarding impulse purchases. This is a brilliant idea for any sort of purchase. Before you decide to make a purchase, sleep on it and wait overnight. You will probably feel differently tomorrow. It greatly reduces impulse buying for things small and large.

This is great advice. But we think it is best for the small purchases. When it comes to a large purchase, we advise going with a 30-day waiting period. Wait 30 days and see if you still need that particular item, or if a cheaper alternative could be found.

A Smarter Smartphone

I have had the same smartphone for a few years. One day, I saw a smartphone that a friend had. It was fancier and cooler than mine, probably even smarter. I decided I needed one. I wanted a new one badly. We had the money, we're not in debt, so it would be okay. Right? Even if the money wasn't earmarked for a new phone, it was there in the bank account waiting to be spent. But I didn't want just any phone, I wanted this fancy smartphone which cost several hundred dollars.

I decided to go to the Apple Store—a bad store to hang out in! I picked it up, played with it and walked around the store trying to justify buying it. Then I looked at my old smartphone and decided I was going to use it for another 30 days before I decided to get a new iPhone because this is our rule. I took my dumber smartphone home, and I really analyzed what the new iPhone could do that my older phone couldn't that would be so valuable to justify paying the extra expense. I really couldn't think of one important difference and decided I would address it again in 30 days.

At the writing of this book, that 30 days passed 5 months ago. I still have the same phone, and it does everything I need. I didn't need a new phone. I was prepared to make that purchase, but because we have the 30-day rule, I needed to wait. It worked.

This same rule can be applied to anything, but it should especially be applied to large ticket items. It's hard the moment you see a good deal on a new couch to not find a hundred ways to justify buying it. But if you wait, you might find that waiting 30 days will make all of the difference. This waiting period will continually save you money. Reality steps in. Financial priorities step in. This is especially important for spenders, like who we used to be.

When you are ready and have thought through your big-ticket purchases, here's how to save:

- Buy used. Buying used will save you 50 percent or more easily. Depending on what the item is, and where you get it, your savings can be even greater! Official resellers are the best route for high-priced electronics, but furniture, simple electronics and other big ticket items are available at thrift stores, in the classifieds and at garage sales.
- Buy refurbished models. Check the reviews of the seller and make sure others have been happy with the refurbished.
- For electronics, if you want new, wait until the new model comes out and buy the previous year's model. This yields instant savings with no extra effort.
- Buy scratch and dent. This is great for appliances and furniture. If you can buy a brand new stainless steel fridge with a small dent and save several hundred dollars, it is totally worth it!
- Buy floor models.
- Save beforehand. Deliberately set the price-point, when you want to purchase and how much you will need to save to purchase it when you desire.
- Depending on what the item is, attempt to negotiate the price at the time of the planned purchase, especially if you find a scratch, dent or flaw.
- Wait for coupon offers and get a percentage off.

As you can see from just scratching the surface above, there are literally hundreds if not thousands of ways to save in all the categories above.

We still have two more major categories to discuss—the household and groceries sections of your budget!

Chapter 13

Trim It Off Slowly Part 3: Grocery/ Household Expenses

By: Cassie

This is one of my favorite chapters to use when playing the 2 percent cut game. You can save so much money in the area of groceries and other household expenses.

Let me start off by stating that this is a huge category and you will find months and months of 2 percent cuts here. It is going to be a category that you will have a lot of wiggle room and have a lot of fun learning tips, tricks and ideas to become more and more creative in saving in the months and years to come.

Savings Tips For Groceries

This is such a broad topic that we could write an entire book just on this section. In fact, we have taught classes and workshops on many topics, but the workshop regarding grocery and food savings ideas is one of our most popular classes. However, we want to provide the basic approach so you can get started in this savings category right away.

Couponing

How to coupon to *actually save money* is different from cutting coupons and going to the store to find the generic is still cheaper than the name brand with coupons.

After you understand the proper couponing concepts, the next step is to implement them. The best time-saving effort is to use coupon match-up grocery shopping lists available online or via shopping apps each week for many of your favorite stores. These lists can be printed off and taken to the store to help you purchase the best deals. The purpose of these lists is to take the store's sale items from the ad that week and combine the sale prices with coupons available right now. This will greatly reduce the time and effort put into couponing.

Each week, we provide coupon match-up sale lists on our site. To find them, visit TheThriftyCouple.com/groceries for the week's current lists at the many stores in your area including grocery stores, drug stores and other stores like Walmart and Target. It's all there.

The information shared to this point provides a brief, but actionable plan for using coupons to actually save money and to use them without consuming so much time. By using these concepts you can save 60 to 80 percent on name-brand packaged foods.

Couponing can be a great tool if you choose to use it to help you save massively on your groceries. Please note it's not the only answer to reap those massive savings, it's just one way to do it.

But our experience and knowledge in this area didn't just stop in the form of couponing, but rather was a very positive stepping stone.

The three tricks of the coupon trade

So just how did I actually have success with couponing? It's a very simple concept, or rather three key tricks of the trade to pull off those super stellar grocery shopping trips.

Here's the quick overview:

- Buy in bulk when an item goes on sale
- Maximize coupons by using only on sale items
- Use multiple coupons to stock up

Buy in bulk

Stores have sales cycles. These cycles are on a rotation, and each of the 10 major companies that produce nearly all the name brand foods and household items run regular sales.

Every 10 to 13 weeks, or about once a quarter, each of these major brands will have a rock-bottom sale. This is the time to buy that company's products and not just buy them, but buy enough to last you and your family until the next rock-bottom sale.

Maximize coupons

Simply buying enough of a product every three months when they are on sale is not the only trick. The other trick is to combine your coupons with that rock-bottom sale. In fact, when you combine those coupons with the rock-bottom sale, you will garner 60 to 80 percent savings in many cases.

Here's an image to illustrate the point.

Understanding Store Prices	
Name Brand	**No Savings** Retail cost is higher than generic
Name Brand (Coupons)	**20–25% Savings*** Generally still more than generic
Generic	**30–40% Savings** Price you want to beat
Name Brand (Sale)	**40–60% Savings** Often less or equal to generic
Name Brand (Combine Sale with Coupons)	**60–80% Savings** Less than generic and great time to buy

Savings based on our experience over years of shopping. All savings amounts are averaged and given in regards to savings off of retail price.

Could you imagine getting your name-brand groceries for 60 to 80 percent off the everyday price? The other trick here is that very often the coupons for products are released a few weeks before a sale, a marketing trick by the industry to weed out the coupon shoppers before the big sales. Instead of using those coupons at just any time, save them and wait for the sales for an even more incredible price.

Here's an example. Let's say our favorite name-brand cereal is $3.49 a box. I have a $0.50 off coupon making it $2.99 a box.

But there is a generic version of our cereal for $2.29 a box. The generic is cheaper.

However, if I wait for a rock-bottom sale on the cereal, like when they have their common $1.99 sales and then I use my coupon, I can get that cereal for $1.49, saving even more than if I had bought the generic.

Using multiple coupons to stock up

Finally, you are going to bring the first two tricks together for a grand finale, stocking up on those 60 percent off or more prices. The way to do that is to have multiple coupons. You can only use one coupon per item or one coupon per the coupon requirements. However, there's no limit, unless the coupon or store places a limit, on how many items you can buy; therefore you can use a coupon for each item.

Using my cereal example, for my family for a three-month time period, I would probably need six boxes of our favorite cereal (because we have cereal about once a week) to get us through until the next rock-bottom sale.

So, I would need six coupons so that I can buy all six at the $1.49 price.

But where would you get that many coupons? The biggest trick for obtaining multiple coupons is purchasing several copies of the Sunday newspaper. Plus there are a myriad of other sources of coupons online and digital coupons from your mobile devices.

Other ways to save on groceries

Today, I still use coupons on occasion, but over the years, I have learned many ways that I can still keep our grocery budget very low and provide healthy, hearty meals for my family.

Here are the ways you can save:

- Stock your pantry with staples like rice, oats, beans, potatoes and flour.
- Make your own bulk muffin mix (recipe in Appendix C) and pancake or waffle mix.
- Blend your own sauces and seasonings for Italian, Asian or Mexican (recipe in Appendix C).
- Make your own cream soups, gravies, cheese sauces and white sauces with the basic sauce or soup (SOS) mix (see page 181).
- Make things from scratch. This saves huge amounts of money, even more than couponing. The time to prepare these items usually takes less time than the time needed for couponing. Plus, you can substitute healthier ingredients to make it much healthier for your family's dietary needs.
- Stock up on meat from local farmers by purchasing in bulk or through a nationwide meat co-op that saves 30 to 50 percent off the top.
- Compare prices on a price sheet (available in Appendix A) to determine your price point so you know when to purchase the remaining items like dairy products when they reach this price point or lower.

Saving money on groceries and food is like building a house. The first step is building the foundation. How do you build a food foundation? This is done by keeping your pantry, freezer and fridge stocked with the basic staples.

We recommend always having a running list of foods that you have on hand at any given time. You can create most any meal out of these basics, and you can replace nearly all grocery store pre-packaged foods and mixes with a healthier, homemade version. It can actually be MUCH healthier when you can control ingredients, use no preservatives and when you can swap ingredients for a healthier counterpart.

We've also included recipes (see Appendix C) for some of these items to get you started. Plus you can stock up and save big on these foods.

Pantry staples to stock up on:

Breakfast
- Oats
- Homemade Pancake/Waffle Mix
- Homemade Bulk Muffin Base (Appendix C)

Lunch/dinner
- Dried or canned beans
- Pasta
- Rice (try a blend of long-grain black wild rice and brown rice).
- Potatoes
- Tortillas
- Flours and grains
- Sugar
- Corn starch
- Baking soda
- Baking powder
- Peanut butter, nut butters and nuts
- Cooking oils
- Vinegar
- Spices
- Homemade mixes like Italian, Asian, Mexican, Ranch and Soup-or-Sauce (SOS) (see page 181)

Some of these staples, like pasta and peanut butter, do have coupons often, but many do not. So here are some quick savings tips on getting staples for less:

- Buy in bulk

- Buy the basic staples above to prepare your own muffins, cakes, pancakes, rice pilafs and macaroni and cheese

- Stock up on these staples items when they go on sale

Here's a list of perishables and quick tips on how to save on those items:

Fruits and vegetables

- Grow your own

- Join a produce co-op

- Shop local farmers markets and produce stands

- Learn to preserve by freezing or canning

- Buy in bulk when in season and freeze

- Buy frozen. Stock up on frozen vegetables and fruits when they are on sale

- Buy markdowns to incorporate into your menu

- Have an end-of-the-week fruit salad with all of your remaining fresh fruits

- Have a stir fry at the end of the week with all of your remaining fresh vegetables

Meats

- Have one to two meatless dinners or lunches per week

- Stock up and freeze the deeply discounted meat on the front page of the weekly grocery ad

- Expand meat proteins with rice or beans

- Buy meats in bulk

- Buy from a meat co-op

Cheese, other dairy and eggs

- Purchase the brand on sale that week

- Keep track of your price point and stock up when the item is cheaper than the price point

- Buy markdown dairy and eggs (see note below)

- Buy butter and cheese in bulk on sale and freeze it

Notes about buying dairy in bulk or on markdown: Many dairy items have a several week out expiration date, but most can also be frozen like cheese (shred or slice before freezing), butter and milk. You can also freeze yogurt if you plan to use it in recipes like smoothies. Eggs can also be frozen raw out of the shell. Our local grocery store is required to put dairy on markdown if it is within 7 to 10 days of the sell-by date.

Bread items
- Make it yourself
- Shop at bakery outlets
- Shop grocery store markdowns two to three days before sell-by dates
- Freeze bulk purchases

Once you have a good foundation of food staples on hand, just keep refilling them as the sales, markdowns and bulk buying opportunities arise.

Now that you have all of these food options, how do you decide what to make on a daily basis? That is where my idea of menu planning comes in. I use online resources to do a quick query on a recipe idea using the odd assortment of ingredients and plan my weekly menu.

Let me tell you . . . This. Is. Awesome! We get to eat a variety of healthy meals, use all of our food and enjoy reaping the massive food savings. I don't shop based on a menu. I make a menu after I have shopped.

This works very well for us, but if you want to create a menu and then shop, we recommend not just picking any menu. The expense will add up quickly with this method! Use a budget-conscious menu plan that works week after week to provide healthy and frugal meals for families. Online menu-based meal plans with shopping lists and recipes for under $5 per meal for a family are widely available. They are designed to keep you under that $5 mark, consistently yielding savings, even when you buy at regular prices.

Savings Tips For Household Items

How about the household category: those items like cleaners, shampoo, toilet paper, toothbrushes, baby diapers and everything in the grocery store that is not edible?

Honestly, this is probably the biggest category of coupon usage for us today. Because I can make healthier, more frugal homemade versions of nearly every packaged food item in the grocery store that has a coupon, I end up using my coupons on this category instead of on food.

Here are some tips that for saving on household items:

- Don't be brand specific. That means that whatever toilet paper, toothbrush, shampoo goes on sale, and you have a coupon, that's the brand to buy that day.

- Use coupons on these items. Combine the sale price with a coupon. Stack the savings with shopping rebate apps.
- Stock up for household essentials at your local drugstore. Drugstore chains have awesome sales, in-store coupons and manufacturer's coupons that can be stacked all together, along with the cash-back rebates and coupons that print at the register at checkout.
- Choose generic options. If you are not brand specific, then generic products are great for household essentials when you don't have a coupon.
- Buy smart. If a coupon is $1.00 off a 12-ounce (360-ml) or larger bottle and the 12-ounce (360-ml) bottle is $2.50 and the 24-ounce (710-ml) bottle is $4.50, get a few bottles of the smaller shampoo for $1.50 instead of paying $3.50 for the large bottle to save an additional $0.50 per bottle. This is one example, but using simple math, comparison and smart shopping, smart savings like this can be found all over.
- Use less. Use economy size bottles to refill smaller bottles. Most people consume less when things are in smaller bottles.
- Make your own cleaners for pennies on the dollar. In Appendix C we have included basic laundry soap, window cleaner, dishwasher soap and all-purpose cleaner recipes that are cheaper than buying manufactured items with coupons and safer for children and pets.
- Make your own homemade personal care items. In Appendix C we share a homemade toner and hand soap recipe to help you start on the basics of homemade personal care. If you prefer natural options for your family you can make your own for much less.

We hope that these chapters have provided some basic money-saving tips and techniques to help you begin your 2 percent monthly decrease journey. We would recommend keeping these money-saving chapters close so that you can quickly refer to the next idea to see if this can be implemented into your home, life and budget.

After you have exhausted these ideas—some of you will already be cutting corners and only may find a couple of months worth of budget cuts here, while for others, this list may last for many, many months—we recommend continually finding new ideas through research, asking friends for ideas on how they save in certain areas, and even reading and following our site regularly as we provide weekly tips on ways to save.

Our Reality Check

When I first started the *extreme-type couponing* early in my money-saving journey, I thought I had reached a peak in my frugality where I could basically walk out of the store paying little to nothing with my super slick couponing skills.

As I have grown in the frugal lifestyle, I realized that this was merely the beginning. Sure, I could get 10 bottles of mustard for free, but in the end, how did this *really* help me reach our family's financial, health and lifestyle goals. Don't get me wrong, couponing is fantastic; it's a high, it's fun, it's addicting, but it's not necessarily the peak of frugality.

In fact, I hardly use any coupons today. I use them mostly for toilet paper and toothbrushes. When I make homemade cleaners, personal care products and homemade foods, it doesn't leave much room for couponing. To me, the results are priceless. My family is much more satisfied with the lifestyle we have now because it is sustainable. There were many times, especially as the extreme couponing world met the real world when couponing rules changed, supply was limited, and if you weren't at the store first thing in the morning the first day of the sale with the other extreme couponers, you missed out. If this was the basis of my grocery shopping, and my budget was dependent on those deals, what would we do?

My family is much more satisfied with the lifestyle we have now because it is healthier. Yes, there are coupons for more natural items. But even then, homemade is healthier, still cheaper, and ultimately easier because you are not counting on those items to be in stock. My family is much more satisfied with the lifestyle we have now because it is simpler. When my pantry is filled with the basic necessities that become the foundation of what we eat and live with, it is a simpler life. It requires less time, less organization, less planning—it's just life simplified! My family is much more satisfied with the lifestyle we have now because it is smarter.

I used to be so proud of myself when I could get fruit snacks for $0.50 a box. But my kids could eat one and still be starving for a real snack. So they would eat two or more and the box would be gone in a flash! This was until the day I became smarter. For example, I realized that bananas were much a smarter option. I can buy a pound of bananas for $0.55 per pound (organic for $0.69 per pound). A pound is about four bananas. That means each banana costs around $0.14 each. A banana actually fills up my kids' tummies when they need a filling, healthy snack, and it leaves them satisfied between meals. That $0.50 box of fruit snacks does not compare in value, health or smarts.

This principle has been applied to many of our buying decisions of late. Sure, we can get *amazing* deals, but is it *smart?* Is it really something I would buy or need *anyway?* If not, I am spending money getting good deals for things that we don't use, need or eat. Therefore, it is just a waste and an example of false economy.

In the end, I have discovered that frugality is not being cheap or being an extreme couponer—it's being real, it's being smart and it's being committed to an overall lifestyle, not just good deals. The frugal lifestyle is a forever journey.

We are always amazed at how much more we learn each and every month. We think to ourselves that we can't get much more frugal or smarter. But, time and time again we learn new things—some are small and some are revolutionary to our lives and our budget. But that's what makes this journey so fun and exciting. It's amazing to see how you grow with your lifestyle.

Chapter 14

How The Money Train Sped Up The Process

By: Cassie

We love this chapter. Why? Because this is the revolutionary chapter that has the potential to quickly increase your debt-payoff strategy.

The chapters presented thus far on making the 2 percent cut to your budget each and every month are life changing, no doubt. Those sustainable changes will help you and your family learn how to live on less while doing so sustainably. What an awesome concept!

But this chapter has even more potential! We recommend that you set your goal to find a 2 percent increase in your income each month. But we have a feeling that your income will increase much, MUCH faster, especially when you implement many of the strategies presented here. Plus, you will one day hit your rock-bottom budget, but the sky is honestly the limit as to your possible income increase.

The concepts presented in this chapter provide a welcome change from the traditional money-making route of going to work day in and day out to put food on the table and a roof over our heads. Instead, the concepts presented below allowed us to become successful business owners and to become financially free in a way that we never expected would happen and wasn't our goal or intent initially.

How can you increase your income by 2 percent each month? That is a great question we hope to answer very shortly.

But first, let's discuss a few things. As we have mentioned before, we are not talking about walking into your boss's office right now and demanding a 2 percent pay increase. We already know that this would probably not work and it's not what we are suggesting.

You could meet your goals solely using the 2 percent monthly decrease and applying that to your debts, and you will get there. But increasing your income by 2 percent each month will help you get there at least twice as fast, if not faster.

This path is different for everyone. We can share general principles and ideas for you to find ways of increasing your income, but we can't tell you exactly what you should do. You and your family are the ones that know your circumstances best and can decide what is going to work for your time, resources and abilities.

You will get smarter. You may start out like we did with a low-paying job, only to realize that you can use your skills and time in a better fashion to make more money in less time.

In the rest of this chapter, you will hear about our money-making journey, along with tips and ideas in case you want to take on a similar approach. Our story merely scratches the surface as to what ideas are available to you and your family.

If you could make an extra $50 a month, how would that affect your budget? What if you could make an extra $100, $200, or even much, much more? We want to plant that question in your mind and give you ideas to help you implement strategic ways that you can increase your family's income to help meet and beat your financial goals.

We are no strangers to finding ways to increase income as we've been working on this for over 13 years. I also grew up in a home where we were constantly working on family projects together to make extra income. My parents didn't have much money, but they found creative ways of making things happen. As a kid, I had so much fun engaging in these income-earning opportunities and then reaping the rewards of our hard work. I may not have picked up on the frugal lifestyle my parents had, but I did pick up on the benefit that comes along with added income. We farmed worms and sold them by the pound, we made and sold crafts, we did yard work for others as a family in all seasons, just to name a few of the many things we did when I was growing up. My family also eventually started an in-home daycare and preschool that my mother ran for many years to pay for my dad's schooling.

By combining a lifetime of experience earning extra income along with our developing frugal skills, we were able to knock out over $90,000 of debt in three years.

The golden ticket in our journey was realizing that in order to get out of the hole and move forward more quickly, we needed to bring in extra income.

But bringing in extra income is such an abstract concept for most people. You do not know how to start. You may also set yourself up for failure by setting an unachievable income goal. You might set expectations that are too high and miss the boat. Then you could get discouraged and frustrated.

We get that.

That's why we want to first give you some tips on how to get started. Then we hope to encourage and help you to set an achievable, realistic standard. We want a standard that can easily be met. This is where the other side of the 2% Rule comes into play.

The idea is to set a reasonable, attainable monthly goal. Then each month, you plan to make 2 percent more than the month before. This is a small enough goal that if you miss it, it's not so discouraging.

When we first started earning extra money, we far surpassed 2 percent! That, of course, is not failure at all. Our first job was delivering newspapers. We brought in about $400 a month—pure gold for us in our desperate time of need!

Then we started realizing that this was labor intensive and required a 4:30 a.m. start EVERY DAY, motivating us to go to the next step, which was delivering phone books. We were paid more, and we could do it when we wanted because there was no set time of day.

This job generated a total of $500 extra per month for two months. This was a very short-term job, but it was enough to help us add to our emergency fund and start catching up on our late bills.

While we were greatly exceeding our 2 percent goal each month with the newspaper and the phone book deliveries, it was exhausting work. It was intended to be temporary to get us out of our rut and quickly build our emergency fund before we attacked our debt.

It was after this that the real work began: finding manageable ways of bringing in extra income without over-taxing our time and our bodies.

Online Selling

I was at home at this point with two kids. I needed to find ways to add to the family's income. This is when I turned to online selling.

I found something that I loved, that I could do from home and that was manageable and scalable. It was also something that if I needed a break, I could take a break and come back to it whenever I wanted. Ideally, you will want to find something you truly enjoy as your extra income stream.

My first attempt at online selling was when I started by selling items around my home that we no longer needed. We had a lot of stuff from our former non-thrifty life! This was a great starting point for me. I was able to pay us the 2 percent increase we had set from what I made monthly, then invest the rest back into the business with the side benefit of clearing out my home!

What did I invest my initial excess into? Well, more stuff, but this time stuff to sell!

Because I had become a super deal hunter through my mad couponing skills, I could find amazing deals on new and used items. I could get new items for much less with coupon stacking on department store items, clothing and shoes. I was able to gain a nice inventory of new items for very little. In fact, soon after I began selling online, I hit a sale for clothing items of all kinds for only $1 each. With my 15 percent off coupon, I got clothing items for $0.85 each. Because I had the money to invest from selling items around my home, I could do this without going further into debt. This is an important point. Going into debt to try to get out of debt does not make sense. I did not stall our payoff plan, and we continued to meet our monthly goals! I was able to turn around my investment and sell name brand clothing in numerous sizes, seasons and styles and make a nice profit.

Shoe Bonanza

Once I hit a buy one, get one half off shoe sale with a coupon for 20 percent off my entire order. I found popular men's athletic shoes on clearance for $5 a pair. They had a couple pairs in each size. With the buy one, get one sale I would pay $7.50 for two pairs, plus the 20 percent off for a final price of $6 for two pairs of shoes. That's $3 per pair. I was fairly confident that I could get at least $10 per pair. So I bought as many pairs as I could. I think I came home with about 10 pairs. Sure enough, I made a nice profit selling them for $8 to $15 each pair!

I also learned to be on the lookout for smart used items like name-brand electronics, movies, games, popular toys and designer accessories at garage sales, thrift stores and the online classifieds. I could make collections of items and sell them in lots. I found lot selling to be much easier as it was much less time on my part, moved the inventory quicker and provided more attractive sales for buyers looking for a collection of like items.

Then, as time went on, I was finding large items to buy for less, but I was not able to sell them online due to shipping costs. So, I began finding items like furniture, big toys and small appliances at garage sales that just needed a good cleaning or small repair. I would take pictures of these products and sell them in local classifieds online for quite a markup! I remember a two-story plastic dollhouse. Someone was selling it at a garage sale for $5. It was dirty. It had pen, pencil and marker marks all over it. I bought it, took it home and spent about an hour cleaning it. It looked nearly brand new! These doll houses were selling for well over $100 new. I listed mine in the free local classifieds online for $50 and ended up selling it that night for $50 after receiving numerous calls! That ONE sale nearly met our 2 percent goal for that month.

I was hooked on selling larger items locally as it was much less work and stress than with the online seller. My average profit margin was 900 percent! This profit margin was much higher than what I was receiving from my online selling.

I ultimately discovered a warehouse in a big city close by that obtains slightly imperfect, overstock or slightly damaged goods from national chain stores. This warehouse would buy these goods by the semi-truck full, then break things down by pallet and auction them off. I began this game and my inventory grew faster than I could sell! What I liked about this source is that everything was new. Although much of it would be junk, there were enough pieces to make the $25 pallet purchase more than profitable.

Selling ended up being quite a profitable endeavor. Plus I could indulge my desire to shop! I was able to use my frugal shopping skills and make money reselling items, investing back into my little business and easily hitting our 2 percent goal each month.

Tips for selling and reselling items

Start with the items you already have at home. One quick idea is to have a garage sale to meet your 2 percent goal the first month, but use any excess to invest back into items for resale.

Next try selling online and in local classifieds. You can even sell using reselling apps for your phone. Simply snap a picture, describe the item and post.

Specialize in buying and selling items specific to your own interests and expertise to maximize your selling profits. For example, my dad sells old, rare and expensive books that he finds at garage sales. He uses an app on his cell phone to determine if items are of good value to resell. It takes him about 15 seconds to check the value.

Contract Work

When we discovered that we were expecting baby number three, it dawned on us that we should be using Alex's skill sets as a software engineer, as I was going to become very busy with baby number three. He reached out to former companies he had worked with and asked if they had any extra tasks, work or needs that required his skills.

Sure enough, one of his former employers was in need of help enhancing a system. Alex contracted to work 10 hours a week at an hourly rate higher than his hourly salary rate. The beauty of contracting is you get paid more per hour than if you are a salaried employee. Yes, you don't receive benefits and extras like a full-time employee, but since he had benefits from his day job, it was pure profit.

This also meant that the 10 hours he worked weekly was bringing in significantly more than the reseller business we operated the previous several months. It was amazing!

There was only one problem with this endeavor. It required Alex to work mostly every night, taking him away from his family time. We determined that this was something that was worth doing so we could temporarily meet that 2 percent income goal, but we both knew it wasn't something he could do sustainably.

The work lasted for a few months and was then complete. From that time forward he kept the part-time consulting option open as we knew it was a great opportunity for more income in small spurts, and he would work on various contracts here and there to do just that. But once our third child was born, we dug deeper and became even smarter.

And it all happened because I was doing what I loved—shopping at the grocery store with my coupons.

Teaching Classes

I had decided to dive back into my reselling business after the birth of our third child. I had thought about babysitting, tutoring and a few other possibilities and dabbled in these a little bit, but I loved the freedom and control over my schedule that my reseller business brought.

I stumbled upon an even bigger plan for me at the grocery store.

A gentleman selling newspapers had a little stand set up, and he stopped me. He taught coupon classes, and he made money by selling the newspaper at his coupon classes to those in attendance.

Would you believe that I agreed to host a class for me and as many of my friends as I could? Of course I did! What did I get for it? Nothing, except a further education in couponing, which was highly valuable to me.

I hosted this class, and I was thrilled to learn even more efficient and better tricks to couponing. My friends were thrilled because they knew of my coupon success and wanted to learn too. This gentleman sold each and every one of us four copies of the newspaper. As he was packing up, he could tell I was itching to know how much he made from those newspaper subscriptions we were all clawing after while he was there. He understood that the coupons were keeping the newspapers in business, and he knew how much they paid in commissions to those who sold subscriptions.

So he started a website where he matched the weekly grocery store deals with the coupons in the newspaper to make for these amazing rock-bottom grocery deals. He provided the lists weekly for free, taught classes for free and sold dozens of newspapers per class.

He just happened to be looking for more people to teach coupon classes. I jumped at this opportunity. It was perfect for me. I loved teaching and sharing with others. Since grocery shopping strategies and tricks with coupons were my current passion at that time, it was a perfect fit for me. I made 100 percent commission on the subscriptions I sold. I averaged about $150 in commission profits per class and I taught classes about two times per week.

How to capitalize on teaching

There are dozens of ways to teach to make money and hundreds, if not thousands of topics you can teach on.

The tried and true method of earning from teaching is the classic tutoring and music lessons model. You can also teach classes locally or online. You can teach a class on ANYTHING from sourdough bread making, to a foreign language, to computer skills, to photography skills, to essential oil usage, to science, literally anything! Record your class using your computer at home, upload it and then charge a fee for your class. It's really a smart idea to earn from your skills and passions all from home!

You can also teach classes in your community advertised through the local colleges or newspapers. You can even teach classes the way I did, by word of mouth, but for any topic! If you have a skill, you can teach a class. I haven't met a person who doesn't have a skill or passion that can be subsequently shared and taught!

Like any work-at-home, side job, it's a broad topic with so many variables, but a little digging, research and passion will help you find a good fit if a teaching type of idea is right up your alley.

Working Online

Working at home was always my goal. Although the coupon classes were partly at home, I wanted to find something that was even bigger, better and even more at home. That is when it became apparent to both of us that a great route could be working at home online.

It was during my coupon class days that one of the gals I taught became a mentor for my next money-making adventure: blogging.

We started our website back in November of 2009 to share our passion for saving money and getting out of debt. The mentor was a money-saving blogger herself. She saw that people kept asking us how we paid off our debts and how we were able to get such great deals. People loved our unique budgeting approach and our 2% Rule for paying off debt. We wanted to reach more people and stop verbally repeating our story over and over again by getting it in writing. We wanted to change the lives of others, just as our plan had changed ours.

That's when she suggested starting a blog. The better news was that it would take minimal investment to start a blog. If we reached enough people, we could start getting paid from advertisers. This seemed like the next logical step! Start a website, share our passions and make money.

Let me be honest, making money as a blogger takes time, patience and a lot of pro bono work upfront. But with diligence, passion and attentiveness you can make a full-time living.

While we worked on our blog and waited for it to make money, I found other online and offline writing assignments that I could get paid for. I also helped other bloggers with tasks and performed various other online tasks through task request sites or with the personal blog connections I had made. This helped provide a bridge income from the time we started operating the blog to when we started actually making money from the website. I also made handmade crafts with my mom and grandma and sold these at shows and online as yet another way to make income on the side.

I remember when we started making $12 a day from our website at TheThriftyCouple.com. It was crazy! Yes, it was less than delivering newspapers at $13 a day, but our efforts were finally paying off after about six months of blogging. It was just a couple of dollars per hour, but it was a great feeling that enough people were visiting and hearing what we had to say for that $12 a day! It just increased from there over the years.

We have also since started a number of other online money-making websites. These additionally support our family and our financial goals. They also secure a strong financial future as we share our passions about finances and frugal living, but also our passion for travel, health and weight loss all through separate websites on those topics.

We started our money-making efforts waking up at 4:30 every single day, delivering newspapers, making $3 per hour. Now, we run full-time businesses from home.

We've shared our money-making journey with you in this chapter, but your story has yet to be told. Your journey is ready to start! Your story can be that of how a little extra income each month for a temporary season in life helped you become debt free or reach another financial goal all the way to the story of becoming a successful, full-time business owner and being your own boss. You can write your story in whatever way you want, all you have to do is start.

You may have a plethora of ideas floating around in your head right now and you don't know where to start. You may have a desire to find something, but don't have ideas.

We have a large section of our site dedicated to helping our readers find ways to generate extra income. We continuously share the latest discoveries and ideas to generate income from home and currently have over 150 ideas and counting.

Chapter 15

The View From 30,000 Feet

By: Cassie

This book is not simply about paying off debt. Yes, that's one step of the process and one that we focus on throughout the majority of this book. But getting out of debt, specifically your consumer debt, is just a single step in building your whole-life financial plan.

One of our main goals for this book is to show you how to use the tool of the 2% Rule to help you pay off your consumer debt. But we also hope that you see that this tool can be used for so much more. It can honestly be used towards meeting each of your financial goals that you and your family will have the rest of your life.

It can be easy to get so caught up in the details of paying down your debt that you lose focus on the need to establish a financial plan for your whole family. That's why we want to share what we refer to as the whole forest picture, or the view from 30,000 feet. There's a reason for each of these steps and even the order that they are presented. Our challenge to you is to find out where you are in the process, jump in and then use the 2% Rule to start attacking that goal.

We really love baby steps. We follow baby steps for many areas of life, and our finances are no exception.

We have presented our baby steps using our 2% Rule to get out of debt followed by many ideas on what to do when you get out of debt. So now we want to lay all of these steps out in order in this chapter so you have a clear process to follow.

There are two important rules to follow when completing these steps. Honestly, the rules are simple and are just common sense. You don't want to go through this process just to continually sabotage yourself. Rules are there to keep us on track.

Those two rules are:

- Rule 1: Stay out of debt.
- Rule 2: Stick with the 2% Rule for life.

I think that these rules are pretty self-explanatory and pretty simple to grasp. Now, it's just a matter of knowing what order of steps to take in your financial life and not only knowing those steps, but what each step entails. Let's take that 30,000 foot view so we can see how this all fits together and where we are headed.

Step 1–Build An Emergency Fund Quickly

When we talked about setting your baseline budget, we mentioned that you are only going to record your regular expenses, not those emergencies like a car repair or the furnace going out. That's where this emergency fund comes in—for those unplanned expenses that are truly emergencies.

This fund is not the FUN-d. It is not for vacations, entertainment, etc. It needs to be saved, set aside and only used for those emergencies.

If there are expenses that only pop up occasionally, like let's say you have a child in a sport and this sport usually requires several hundred in equipment/uniform, that needs to be part of your budget. As we said previously, the emergency fund is not for that. This is for car repairs; home repairs that are not part of a home improvement project; and any other real, unexpected emergency.

The first step is a critical one. I am going to present a bit of a paradox compared to what we have presented to you thus far in this book.

What is that paradox?

We've been talking about and promoting the idea behind gradual changes and progress as this equals far greater success and a better chance of lifelong success.

However, when it comes to the emergency fund, we recommend that you make some major sacrifices to build this up FAST!

We truly believe in implementing gradual, sustainable change over the long run so you don't burn out or return to your prior way of life when your current financial goal is completed. However, the idea for the emergency fund is that you can make major lifestyle changes for a short period to free up some cash fast. Plus, we don't want you to get caught up in this step, but complete it quickly so you can start seeing success in the overall plan.

Complete this step as quickly as you can, generally in 30 days or less.

As mentioned earlier, we recommend that your emergency fund is based on 1 to 2 percent of your gross annual income. Plan on 1 percent at the minimum and then evaluate past years' emergencies, frequency and potential upcoming issues you might already know about. If you deem that these emergencies are likely to happen, increase your fund to 2 percent of your gross annual income.

Thus, if you are making $50,000 as a household, you will want to have $500 to $1,000 in an emergency fund. If you are making $100,000, you will want $1,000 to $2,000 in an emergency fund.

If at any time you end up using funds from your emergency fund, take a few weeks and build it up fast again.

You need to maintain the 1 to 2 percent minimum through the entirety of Steps 2 through 4 below.

Emergency Funds In 30 Days

Thirty days may not seem like a long enough time period, but to the surprise of many, with a bit of effort it can come together, even when you think you have nothing. Here are some of our top ideas to help get you started:

- Have a penniless week. What is a penniless week? For 7 whole days, you act and live like you literally do not have a penny to spend. We say only 7 days because it is hard to go beyond that. Other than filling your car with gas *just for work*, don't spend a penny for the whole week. Eat everything in your cupboards and fridge at home and find free entertainment, minimize driving and whatever else you can do for the week. Don't make up for it before or after, just go about life as normal so that the money saved is truly *money saved*. The end result for most households has been between $300 and $500.
- Sell old cell phones, music players, tablets and other electronics online to electronic sellers. A quick search will produce the current offers. You might be surprised about how many devices you have to sell and how much money you can collect with this process.
- Sell old textbooks, books, movies, video games or music discs to Amazon on the Amazon buy-back program. Even if you didn't buy your items on Amazon, you can sell them to Amazon for cash. It's a very easy process that yields some fast cash.
- Clean out your house and have a garage sale. Sell more expensive or larger items on local classifieds for a higher selling price. You will reap the side benefit of a cleaner house too.

- If you have unused gift cards, sell them to gift card reseller sites and get 90 to 95 percent of the gift card value back in cash.
- Offer some services or tasks to friends, family and neighbors for a month (mowing lawns, snow shoveling, weeding, errands, organizing, cleaning). There are literally hundreds of little tasks that you can charge per hour or per task. One great idea for stay-at-home moms is offering an errand-day babysitting service for moms in your neighborhood; have the drop-off service one day a week for a month or even just one time saying they can drop their kids off for the day or afternoon to take care of tasks and charge per hour per kid. It's a fast way to make money without a long babysitting commitment.
- As a more extreme measure if you need a bit more after the above steps, consider donating plasma for a month. On average, one person can earn $240 over a month and a couple can earn $480.

All of the above tips also do not consider any money you may have left over after paying all of your bills. Many of you may not be as far in the red as we were when we started. We had to find the money somewhere else besides our leftover income since there wasn't any. If you are in a better place than where we started you may have some of this to take into account for the month!

Step 2—Pay Off All Consumer Debt Using The 2% Rule

This is really a critical step: dump the debt.

We have been asked about our best investment strategy. Odd as it may seem, our primary strategy is to pay off your debt as we have found that the interest on a family's total debt load usually exceeds by far any amount of money made on an investment. Rarely does a scenario happen where tying up money in investments is more profitable than paying off your debts.

Not only is it a wiser investment of your money, but also the peace of mind and financial freedom you will experience is unsurpassed . . . priceless! As you read our story, you will note the emotional turmoil that debt brought into our lives.

The main point of this book is to ditch the debt. With that, we have presented our 2% Rule and detailed the specifics and application of the plan on an ongoing monthly basis.

This first step will be the longest step for most people and that is perfectly fine. It's the most important step and the fundamental, first step that will help transform your mindset and change your life.

Implement the plan and see the results!

Step 3–Set Up Biweekly Mortgage Payments Immediately

If you have a mortgage, we recommend getting this next step in place. We talk about this more in Chapter 18 (page 154), but it is a smart, brainless and painless way to knock off several years and tens of thousands in interest.

A biweekly payment system pays half a mortgage payment every two weeks instead of one whole payment once a month. Since there are 52 weeks in a year, this equals 26 half payments, which is 13 full payments. On the typical system now, you are making 12 full payments a year. So this biweekly system makes one extra full payment a year. Verify that your extra payment is applied towards principal. Over just a handful of years, the average homeowner can save about $50,000 in interest and shorten their payoff period by seven years.

A side benefit of biweekly mortgage payments is that your paychecks will have a more even distribution monthly, which ultimately helps your budgeting and living all around. When you have a once monthly mortgage payment, one paycheck a month typically has nothing left over after making that mortgage payment, while the other paycheck seems to have a big surplus. Instead, when you implement a biweekly mortgage system, your leftover amount for each paycheck will be far more equal.

Step 4–Contribute The Maximum On Your 401(k) For Company Match

It's time to take extra steps in saving for retirement. Remember that we mentioned in Step 2 that the smartest investment strategy is to become debt free. There will rarely be an investment that will have a better return on investment than the interest you are paying on your debts.

Once you have paid off your debt, however, it's time to start considering the steps you can take to invest in your future. One low-hanging fruit that you won't want to miss is funding your 401(k) up to the percent that your company will match so you don't miss out on that free money from your employer.

We'll go into more depth on this step in Chapter 17 (page 149).

Step 5–Build 3 To 6 Months Of Savings

Now that you are debt free, have implemented the biweekly mortgage payments and are contributing enough into your 401(k) to maximize the company match, it is time to have a bigger savings nest egg for bigger emergencies, life changes and unplanned events.

As life goes on, your emergencies and unplanned life-events become even more likely. The 1 to 2 percent emergency fund is a low, base minimum to keep your head above water. But it is not going to cover you in cases of lost jobs, a move, medical emergencies or any other big event that life throws your way.

It is never going to hurt you to have a nice savings account balance. Best case, you have a nice savings account. Worst case, you have quite a bit more money to live off of or to use in a bigger emergency, greatly reducing your risk of needing to go into debt to get you out of that emergency.

We recommend you save enough to cover at least three months of expenses, but an optimal amount is six months of expenses. As with the emergency fund, if you have to dip into this savings account, replenish it as soon as you can to be prepared for the next life event.

Step 6–Contribute The Remaining Retirement 15% Into A Roth IRA

After fully funding your 401(k) to your company's match, we suggest investing the remaining 15 percent of your income into a Roth IRA to meet your recommended 15 percent retirement goal. If you are ready for this then feel free to review those details and more in Chapter 17 (page 149).

Step 7–Set Up Your Cash And Percentage-Based Savings And Add Your Contributions

This is a big and important step, keeping you out of debt and on track to be able to afford what you need in the future and pay cash for it. Note that this step is different from the three to six months of savings, as that emergency fund is only intended for emergencies. This step is your savings account for your next family vacation or your next vehicle.

We use what we coined as percentage-based finances, essentially laying out what percentage of your pay will be reserved for certain parts of life. Chapter 16 (page 143) details the concepts behind percentage-based finances and gives suggestions on how to apply the percentages to each category. These are savings accounts/categories for long-term goals, not for your everyday monthly expenses like groceries, clothing or eating out. This step allows you to save and plan for those future expenses.

This step is ongoing. You will always be funding these categories. It is such a blessing to have a nice vacation nest egg, a nice home improvement nest egg or a nice Christmas fund for the rest of your life!

Step 8–Contribute The Maximum Household Allowance For A Roth IRA

Now that you are saving for the major areas of life, it is a great time to implement the next smart investment strategy for retirement.

After you have determined your cash and percentage-based savings needs by category from Step 7, the next step we suggest is to take full advantage of your maximum annual contributions to a Roth IRA.

At the writing of this book, the maximum Roth IRA annual contributions are $5,500 per year, per person which means $11,000 per married couple split between two separate Roth IRA accounts. We encourage you to invest and maximize that $5,500 per person.

This portion can also be used as a strategic savings account for some of your longer-term savings goals from Step 7. We will be sharing the ideas and details behind the Roth IRA investment strategy in Chapter 17 (page 149).

Step 9—Round Mortgage Payments To The Nearest $100

I love this step because it is so incredibly simple and yields a huge return on investment! Not only does this idea save you a ton of money in mortgage interest, it brings you many steps closer to becoming a real homeowner.

No matter your payment plan for your mortgage, simply round up the current payments to the nearest $100 amount.

By doing this, you will knock off an average of another several thousand dollars of interest and be several years closer to owning your home outright.

In Chapter 18 (page 154), we will show you why this is a smart step!

Step 10—Fund Businesses

This next step may not apply to everyone, but if you own a business of any kind, investing into your business could yield a higher return than most investments. The point is that businesses often require money to make money. In this step of the process, it requires *more* money to make *more* money.

This was a surprising step for us. One weakness we discovered along our path, after becoming debt free and running side businesses, was that we had become frugal in life, which led us to be frugal in business. We did have a few years of very slow growth because we were very austere with our business funds, which ultimately hurt us. We couldn't accomplish everything we needed to do to run the business, but we were too cheap to hire anyone to help. We also were too cheap to invest in tools and resources that would have tremendously helped our business.

Once we decided that we needed to invest more back into our business by following a similar 2 percent plan, growth started happening at a much faster rate. So, consider investing more into your businesses. Be a wise and shrewd manager and business owner, but seriously consider your business needs and investments.

Step 11—Pay Extra Towards Mortgage

Surprise, surprise. We are back on the mortgage idea. Again, the mortgage is a great place to invest extra money because you are going to have the final result of a real property investment. Yes, it might not be generating cash flow when it's paid off like other investments could, but not having a mortgage payment one day in the future will provide much more financial freedom and ability to make more risky investments.

Plus, paying anything extra at all is going to give you a huge return on your investment in this area by saving you loads of money in interest and greatly reducing your payoff time.

We really want to encourage you to invest in your home. It is one of the least risky investment options out there. So these little extra steps are going to get you closer to that goal.

Step 12–Implement The 7-10 Mortgage Plan

Finally, the last concrete step is to fully implement the 7–10 mortgage plan. What is the 7–10 mortgage plan? Well, I actually don't want to share the secret in this chapter but will let you read more about it in Chapter 18 (page 154). It is a very exciting and freeing chapter.

It may take time after funding the other categories for you to get to this stage. For others, you may reach this step very quickly. It really doesn't matter how slowly or how quickly you get here. All that matters is that when you get to this point, you understand that you are already in an amazing place, especially when compared to the average household. Getting to this step is beyond commendable—it's amazing!

Then once you hit this point, it will seem like smooth sailing to declaring total financial independence as you speedily and quickly pay off your mortgage!

Step 13–Decide Your Next Financial Investments And Steps

When you reach Step 13, you have accomplished some absolutely incredible financial feats! When you reach the end of this book, you will realize just how possible this life-long financial strategy is, especially with the 2% Rule.

When it comes to Step 13, this is the time for you to pick up our next book or the latest book on investment strategies and decide where you want your future to be heading. Each strategy you implement should always come from that extra 2 percent you gain each month and in no way bring you back into debt. Be careful that you don't allow your investment strategy to stretch you so thin that you find yourself back in a lifestyle of taking out loans and needing to live in a manner inconsistent with what the rest of this book has been attempting to show you. In the end, allow your investment strategy to come from an amount over and above your living expenses so you have a wise and sustainable investment strategy for your future.

Now that I have laid out the 13 steps, it's time to begin or continue your amazing journey. We cannot wait for you to turn the pages of this book and see these steps come to life. The next step is your own—to follow these steps to change your life!

Chapter 16

Two Percent To Life

By: Alex

We hope you haven't lost sight of one of the most important points throughout all of our stories and tips we've shared over the last several chapters. Obviously one of the most important goals throughout this process has been to pay off your debt or meet other financial goals. But another main goal throughout all of this has been to do it sustainably each step of the way.

What we're encouraging is that each 2 percent cut and every 2 percent increase should not be viewed as sacrifices that you're having to make for a short term with the plan to go back to life as normal after you meet your goals. Instead, these changes should all be viewed as steps made towards a new lifestyle.

Do you see the beauty behind this? Instead of becoming the next "got out of debt" statistic that goes back to their prior lifestyle, our plan is different. This new life allows you to do exactly what we've shared along the way. Like we mentioned, what we live on now as a family of eight is actually *less than* what we lived on years ago as just the two of us.

The next steps are even better. Hopefully, at this point living by the 2% Rule has become a matter of habit and maybe also a game. When in the past you might grimace at the thought of having to find another 2 percent cut or grudgingly try to come up with the next way you're going to try to find the next 2 percent increase in your income, it's all changed now. What was difficult before has now become a new challenge that you look forward to accomplishing. The family looks forward to another month with more potential to drive up the income by just that much more!

Yes, it's when you get to this point that you realize that the point of this book has been not only to get you to pay off your debt, but to do so in a way that ultimately changes your life for good! It's at this point that we also hope you see paying off your debt was only a stepping stone to your next financial goal, and then your next.

No matter where you are in life, there will be no lack of financial goals. Sure, you paid off your vehicle, but what about your future car? After all this work, you don't want to go right back into debt, just to start this process all over, do you? Instead, you might see that saving up for your next car becomes a lot easier when you don't have debt. Remember all that money you were throwing at your debt at the end of your debt-free journey? Now that can be saved up for the next goal.

What about saving up another three to six months of funds in case you lose your job and need to rely upon that savings to get you through until you find another job? What if you even wanted to transition one of those supplemental income sources into your next full-time method of making money? Isn't it easier to now understand how quickly you can set that money aside and prepare for that worst-case scenario?

What about your house? Do you see how additional money can now be applied to your mortgage with the goal of paying it off in half the time, or even less, than you had originally planned? Just think of all the interest and money you'll save by paying your home off early.

Don't forget about putting the kids through college and beyond with retirement looming just a few years after. All of these goals become a greater reality and easier to reach once you are free of your consumer debt, but even more so in a sustainable way that will result in a successful transition to the next part of your 2 percent financial plan.

All of a sudden, a sense of peace and freedom should settle upon you because you've gotten to the point that 2 percent is just a way of life. You can tell that life is going to be different now.

That's the joy of living the 2 percent life!

Preparing For The Worst

Before implementing the percentage-based finances below, you need to have three to six months of your necessary budget expenses in savings in case the worst happens. At this point, having your debt paid off is a freeing feeling, isn't it? The emergency savings of approximately three to six months of expenses gives you the buffer you need in case you lose your job or primary income so you don't have to go back into debt.

With where you ended rolling all the excess payments forward from your debt payoff strategy, we hope you see that it may not take as long as you initially expect to fill that account. Sit down with your family, determine what that amount is that would be sufficient and start the plan immediately.

Percentage-Based Finances

Now we wouldn't be The Thrifty Couple if we didn't share with you the tips and tools you can use to take the next step in living the 2 percent life. This ties in with our encouragement to Be Intentional (see Chapter 20) in every area of your life, but especially in the area of your finances.

It can become easy to have this extra money come in to your home and give little thought or consideration to where it should be allocated. If that money doesn't have a purpose as soon as it comes in the door, the greatest temptation might be to dream of trips, cars or more!

It is time for you to specify the next set of financial needs and address them first.

That's what this next section is about: being intentional by giving your dollars a name and ensuring that your needs are met and that your future financial plans are being saved for, all before you start spending wildly. All of this happens before the money even comes in the door, because you have already planned ahead and decided where it should go.

To plan and decide where the money should go, we used what's called percentage-based finances. In a nutshell, it's a process of assigning a percentage of your income to specified categories. The actual percentages you need might be different based on your specific family's needs. The important part is that in the end, we hope you take some of the categories we recommend and decide how they fit into your plan.

Before we begin

We want to share why we like percentage-based finances versus straight dollar amount finances.

As you continue to increase your income at the rate of 2 percent per month, you'll see that the money you have at your disposal grows as well. Likewise, on months where you didn't quite hit your 2 percent increase, or worse, your income dropped due to a slow time for your business, you'll find that setting aside a percentage will be a much easier way to track what you allocate to your different accounts to plan for a more secure financial future.

For those months where you didn't quite make the additional amount, instead of trying to set aside money you don't have this month, the percentage-based approach simply allows you to adjust what you save based on reality. This helps to decrease your stress during leaner times, but still keeps you on track.

Additionally, budgeting those funds using the percentage-based approach allows those accounts to grow faster. When you are trying to save money for something a bit more abstract like a child's college expenses or your future retirement, each additional dollar saved today will become that much more valuable later when you need it. Using a percentage-based approach may also help you surpass whatever goal you might have set with a straight dollar-based approach.

So let's take a look at a sample percentage-based approach towards life to give you an idea of how to proceed. Remember, these are guidelines. Each family must consider their own set of variables in setting up percentages.

Sample percentage based savings categories for household

- Giving: 5 to 15%
- Christmas: 1%
- Vacation: 3 to 4%
- Home improvement: 5 to 15%
- Car: 5 to 15%
- College: 5 to 10%
- Retirement: 15 to 20%

Here are some questions you can ask to help determine the right percentage for you and your family as you prepare to set up these categories:

Giving

- What charities do you want to give your money to?
- Is there a set amount you want to donate to those specific charities?
- Are there certain charities that you don't normally consider but want to set money aside for now to give at a different time of the year? These could be seasonal charities or others that target their donations during special days.

Christmas

- Based on your values and what you want to provide for your children, how much would you like to have set aside by Christmas to enjoy it debt free?
- What are the ages of your children? Families with younger children might find it easier to set aside less money than families with older children due to the cost of certain gifts, etc.
- How many are you buying for? Obviously when you have more people in your family you might find it necessary to set aside a higher budget.
- Do you have any traditions that require you to have extra money set aside?
- Would you like to spend a bit more this year to celebrate the family's dedication to paying off your debt over the last few years?

Vacation

- How many people are in your family that you would be taking?
- What type of vacation are you saving for? A road trip will obviously be much cheaper than flying your family cross-country on a trip to Disney World.
- How many days and nights?
- When we determine the current/upcoming year's vacation, we create sample itineraries and obtain sample package quotes so that we have a worst-case basis for how much a potential vacation will cost to work towards saving. Then, as the vacation draws near, using our travel tips, we can generally book each aspect of the vacation at a much lower rate than first quoted. This process ensures we save enough, rather than too little.

Home improvement

- How old is your current home? How old are your appliances? Older homes and appliances might require additional savings to prepare for various maintenance and/or new appliances.
- Are you hoping to finish your basement? Do you have any other large or small planned improvements that you need to save up for?
- What have you been spending on repairs over the past year(s)? There's definitely a good amount of wisdom that you can often prepare for the future by looking at your past.
- Do you have any need of furniture in the near future that would require a higher percentage?

Car

- How many vehicles are you needing to replace?
- Do you have specific needs for your vehicles?
- Are you looking to buy a newer used car or older used car?
- What type of repairs do you foresee for your current cars?

College

- How many children and their current ages, do they plan to attend school?
- Depending on your children's current skills and desires (a child that expresses they want to join the armed forces or skip college might not require a college savings or less of it).

Retirement

- Many financial experts recommend setting aside at least 15 percent of your income for retirement at minimum. But the amount of money you desire to have available to you at retirement could greatly affect this percentage.

As you can see, there are many different variables that could affect the total amounts you hope to set aside for your family's budget. The ideas above are just a starting point. Sit down with your spouse and children to consider each of these categories, and brainstorm for other questions and variables you might need to consider to set your percentages.

The main point we want to stress is to *be intentional*. Once you have decided the reasoning behind what you set aside and the amounts tied to that reasoning, you can then take the next step and intentionally set that money aside.

As soon as you receive your paycheck or income, immediately set aside those percentages before even thinking about it. The wisest words are borrowed from Cassie's favorite game, Monopoly: "Do not pass go. Do not collect $200. Go directly to…" Yes, set aside those funds before they get warm in your checking account, before you get used to seeing that balance higher than you are accustomed. Set those funds aside just as soon as you can so you are not tempted to spend them somewhere else.

An additional step to ensure that the funds set aside are allocated for the intended purpose is to set up multiple savings accounts. If you bank online, you can manage these accounts from your computer at home and transfer the funds from your primary account into your allocated savings. This makes it more manageable, easier to see the goals being met and harder to use the funds other than for the intended purpose.

In the end, you tell your money where to go. As soon as you do, you'll notice that you and your family will continue on track towards meeting your next financial goal, whatever it might be. The next chapter will also dive a little deeper into other ideas for longer-term savings to maximize interest and return rates to get more out of your money.

We hope you see just how valuable living the 2 percent life can be towards your family's future and not just towards paying off your debt. This plan is created with the goal in mind to help everyone's plans, no matter the goal.

Chapter 17

Investments For The Rest Of Us

By: Alex

This book is not meant to give you instructions on how or where you should invest your money. We don't claim to be experts in investments, and have much to learn ourselves. However, we have learned a few strategies and concepts along the way that we would be remiss not to share with you now.

Let's get started with our five-step, high-level overview of investing and preparing not only for your retirement, but also for other shorter term investments.

Invest In Your 401(k) Up To The Company Match

If you get nothing else from this chapter, make sure to read this section. You don't want to be giving up free money. What are we talking about?

Have you ever dreamed of walking into your boss's office and asking for a 3 percent increase in pay and receive it without your boss even blinking an eye?

What we're talking about is the employer match offered with many 401(k) plans at your work. In case you don't know, the 401(k) is a company sponsored, pre-tax retirement plan that allows you to contribute a percentage of your earnings into a fund that will grow using mutual funds, company stock and more. Once you reach 59½, you can start withdrawing those funds. The funds you withdraw are then taxed according to your tax bracket the year they are withdrawn.

The employer match is a benefit that many, but not all, employers offer as an incentive and bonus. The match may differ from company to company, but it is generally about 3 percent. The company will match your contribution up to the maximum match. That means if you invest

3 percent of your pre-tax income into the fund, the company will contribute the same amount into the fund, often in the form of company stock.

Let's take a look at a simple example to help you understand this point. If you happen to make $50,000 annually and decide to contribute the full 3 percent, you would be investing a total of $1,500 into your 401(k) account. Your company would then invest an additional $1,500 with a total of $3,000 invested that year in your 401(k).

However, let's be very clear. If you only invested 1 percent of your income, your company would only match 1 percent. This means you would miss out on 2 percent of the total benefit your company is offering, which in our example with $50,000 income would mean $1,000 in missed contribution. Obviously if you didn't invest anything towards your 401(k), you would be missing out on the full 3 percent match, or $1,500.

When you either don't invest up to the match, or worse don't invest at all, you are throwing away free money. You might argue that you are still having to invest the full $1,500 yourself. That's true, but we encourage you to very seriously consider what you are doing now to prepare for retirement.

Finally, when considering your 401(k), be aware that leaving your company before becoming fully vested in your 401(k) might result in losing part or all of that company match.

Don't forget to check your 401(k) plan as soon as you can and make sure you're not leaving money on the table by not investing up to the match. Even if you're in the middle of the year, you should be able to talk to your human resources department to get that resolved and start getting that free money today.

Invest In A Roth IRA

The next step towards a successful investment strategy is to open and invest in a Roth IRA. The Roth IRA is an Individual Retirement Account (IRA) named after Senator William Roth who was the main sponsor of its establishment in the late 1980s.

The Roth IRA allows you to invest up to a certain amount ($5,500 per person, per year at the time of this writing) of post-tax dollars. Once invested, the capital gains you earn in that account will never be taxed unless the earnings are withdrawn prior to age 59½.

There are so many advantages to this investment account that we can only name a few in the limited space we have here.

First, because you have already paid taxes on the contribution, you can withdraw them at any time without any tax penalty. The earnings cannot be withdrawn without penalty, but the contribution can. This sets it apart from the standard pre-tax IRA contribution. If an emergency happened where you needed access to additional funds, you could use this money. In fact, the next strategy will address a little known investment option that is available because of this fact.

Unlike other retirement accounts, there is no mandatory age at which you must start withdrawing funds from these accounts. So, if you have other investments or income that you are able to use in retirement, you can keep that Roth IRA untouched and even bequeath it to your dependants without ever making a withdrawal.

We also love the fact that married couples are allowed to have two accounts, or rather one for each person, up to an investment total of up to $11,000 per couple per year. This allows you to really start seeing your retirement grow.

What we recommend and do ourselves is to fund your 401(k) *up to* the percentage that earns your company match and then turn to the Roth IRA. This allows you to have access to your money if ever needed and all at a tax-free withdrawal when you need it one day.

Use your Roth IRA for short-term investments

Now this may seem counterintuitive to what we just shared in the last section, but due to the ability of a Roth IRA to allow you to withdraw your contributions at any time—again, not the interest or capital gains—there's a nice investment strategy you can use when saving for those larger purchases.

For example, let's suppose you are saving $300 per month towards your next vehicle. You can place that money into a savings account, but at the standard rates today of 0.01 to 0.05 percent interest, it's about the same thing as putting the money under your mattress except that it will be a bit safer in case your house is robbed.

Instead, suppose you have invested into your 401(k) up to the company match per our first investment strategy, but are only able to invest another $2,000 into a Roth IRA. Suppose you could put that $300 into a Roth IRA in a low-risk fund, that interest rate would theoretically be a bit higher by a few percentage points.

Now obviously, you need to be very careful with the type of fund you place that money in as you are counting on the need to withdraw those funds probably sometime in the next two to three years, but if you are careful about the type of fund and can accept a small amount of risk, you can easily see how the interest you gain by placing it into the Roth IRA makes more sense from an investment strategy standpoint.

For example, let's say you put that money into a 1-year Certificate of Deposit (CD) at an interest rate of about 1 percent. Assuming an inflation rate of 3 to 4 percent, you are still losing money but your rate of return is 20 to 100 times that of the savings account referred to above. If you chose a bit higher risk for that fund, your hopeful rate of return would be much higher!

Now there are a few considerations of course. The interest that you earn cannot be taken out of the account tax-free until you are 59½. So this example assumes you aren't trying to earn the interest for use now, but rather to keep it in the Roth IRA to allow you to continue to build towards retirement.

In addition, you need to consider the time you will need to get those contributions out of your Roth IRA. If you want to use that invested money for a purchase, you will need to submit the request weeks before you need the money to use for your desired purchase.

Lastly, please hear us. Our goal would be for your Roth IRAs to be fully funded and growing towards your retirement. This investment strategy is specifically for those that aren't fully maxing out those funds each year and are trying to find a place to store funds they are saving towards their next large purchase.

Invest In Your business

As you continue your quest for 2 percent to life, we assume you will continue to build upon your own income strategies each month as you grow in your passion, your level of knowledge and skill and ability to make money. All in all, you may get to a point where you foresee your part-time income that you used to get out of debt turning into something larger, even to the point of replacing your full-time income.

Please don't think that to be successful in either paying off your debt or having a successful investment strategy that you are required to turn your short-term income sources into full-time jobs. However, if you happen to do so, then this section is for you.

We have learned that when someone is passionate about their own business, that passion will often result in success. The blood, sweat and tears spilled in those initial years often are turned into dollars and growth. We're not saying that this happens all the time, but a certain level of passion and zeal does help a business owner go further and get bigger than an owner just hoping to make a profit.

With that, you might want to consider investing a certain amount of your income after your 401(k) and Roth IRA into your home business. Knowing the truth of the adage, "It takes money to make money," a little extra investment from you just might give you what you need to go the extra step.

Be careful, invest wisely and don't put all your eggs into one basket! That said, once you have invested into your retirement funds and assumedly any education fund for your children, it will be up to you to determine how much you want to put into your business.

Read

Again, this book was never intended to be your go-to investment manual.

One reason for that is that we are still growing ourselves in this area of our lives. We are currently implementing the strategies you read here and plan to expand our knowledge greatly over the next few years. Honestly, it's been a few years since we paid off our consumer debt, but we are still more green than we would like to admit in the area of investing.

If you are looking for a deeper dive into the world of investing, we encourage you to read from many sources and to drink from them deeply.

But be careful that each strategy you implement should always come from that extra 2 percent you gain each month and in no way bring you back into debt. Be careful that you don't allow your investment strategy to stretch you so thin that you find yourself back in a lifestyle of taking out loans and needing to live in a manner inconsistent with what the rest of this book has been attempting to show you. In the end, allow your investment strategy to come from an amount over and above your living expenses. At that point you will have a wise investment strategy and one that is sustainable for your future.

Chapter 18

THE 7-10 MORTGAGE PLAN
BY: CASSIE

If you have made it this far with us in our book, we know you are excited and fully motivated to put this whole plan to live debt free and financially sound for life into place. You have also arrived at one of our favorite parts of our journey where we discuss the plan to be an *actual* homeowner!

What do we mean by this? Most people have the misconception that by signing documents at closing and securing their first mortgage they are a homeowner. Not so! Having a mortgage means that a person has a loan to purchase the home, but the financial institution is the actual owner until that last penny has been paid off.

Our goal for this chapter is to help *you* get to the point where you can take that last penny to the bank and become a real homeowner.

Once you reach the point in your financial journey where you can actually start paying down your mortgage, and ultimately pay off your home, is an amazing time! It makes all the hard work and sacrifice up to this point completely worth it. Being a real homeowner is one of the greatest achievements in a financial journey!

This is a rich, rich chapter filled with easy steps, tricks and strategies to knock that mortgage payment to the curb and knock it out fast. And it won't be as painful as you think.

Up to this point, using the steps and tips we've shared through this process, you have been making small, incremental changes at a rate of 2 percent. What this has provided along the way is the opportunity to pay off your debts at a manageable rate for ensured success and a long-term lifestyle of wise financial decisions.

At the end of paying off all of your debts, meeting the other financial goals outlined in Chapter 16 with the percentage-based finances and the investment opportunities, you should be at a point (barring any emergencies in life or drastic work changes) that you can attack your mortgage. Only start this after your consumer debt is paid, and all your investments defined in the last chapter are completely funded. We want all of these categories to still be fed at the rates we talked about in the previous chapters. We don't want you to abandon any of these to focus on just the mortgage. This could potentially set you up for failure.

You need to keep these other categories running and going just as we have discussed in previous chapters. But here's where the cool part comes in. Once you are at this point you can potentially cut the time to pay off your mortgage in half without much more sacrifice.

You can even accomplish this faster with harder work and more sacrifice, especially if you have found yourself consistently bringing in more than 2 percent increase in income each month. Perhaps you have stopped or greatly decreased the extra money-making opportunities after paying off your debts. At this time you'll need to consider whether you want to jump back into the money-making plan for the next few years to attack your mortgage.

Whatever the case may be, if you look through your budget at the moment, you may well find a decent surplus left over after paying your utilities and other monthly, non-debt bills and after funding your retirement, your other investments and education funds each month.

In fact, there is a good chance that your previous total debt payments were equal to or surpassed that of your current mortgage payment. If that is the case, you may well be able to make a double mortgage payment.

As you may remember, at the end of our debt payoff, we were paying $4,500 a month. When our debt was paid off, that became our surplus. For us, that $4,500 far surpassed our mortgage payment. After feeding our retirement, IRAs and disbursing the remaining funds using our percentage-based finances, we still had a fair amount of money monthly that we could assign to paying off the mortgage.

Think about it. Go back through your worksheets that you completed throughout the course of this book and you may find that your total debt-load of payments came close to or surpassed your mortgage payment.

At this point, you should be at your rock-bottom budget and spending wisely along with bringing in extra income. So you will be far ahead of where you were when you started this journey.

The 7–10 Mortgage Plan

The plain and simple explanation of the 7–10 mortgage plan is that if you can make a double mortgage payment, you will pay off your home in 10 years on a 30-year loan and 7 years on a 15-year loan.

How does the 7–10 mortgage plan work?

It's very simple! If you have a 15-year loan, double your payments and you will have it paid off in less than half the time, just under 7 years.

If you have a 30-year loan, double your payments and you will have it paid off in a little more than one-third of the time, just over 10 years.

The math works very simply. No matter what your balance is, no matter how much your house cost, no matter what your payment, double your payments and you will reach these totals!

It's All In The Numbers

Let's do some math. The average mortgage payment in America is $1,061.

The average consumer debt in America per household is $1,203.21.

Let's break that down reviewing the average monthly payments with average monthly rates:

Credit Card Debts = (higher payment of 2 percent balance at 14 percent average rate) = $305.46 per month

Student Loans = $37,172 (10-year term at average of 6 percent rate) = $416.85

Auto Loans = $30,738 (average of a six year loan with lower interest of 4 percent) = $480.90 per month

Total = $1,203.21 in monthly consumer debt payments.

That means that the average household is paying more in non-mortgage debt than their actual mortgage. This was more than true for us. We were paying as much in interest as our mortgage payment, let alone our total debt payments! So, with the debt gone, the above example shows how easily the average household can double a mortgage payment even before considering the 2 percent spending decrease and 2 percent income increase each month.

Compare what you were paying in total monthly payments at the height of your debt pay-off plan? Now think about it again. Does the double payment seem more plausible now?

Just think if you applied the 7–10 plan to the best of your abilities with the end result of no mortgage. Think about how you will feel and how much you will have EVERY MONTH when that mortgage payment is GONE!!

Let us try to seal the deal with you to show you some shocking numbers. Remember, the average household makes enough total debt payments to surpass that of their mortgage payment. Let's share some examples of the impact paying your home off can have for your finances and your life.

First, we are going to use the average home price as shared previously of $284,000. If you put $0 down, received an average interest rate of 4.5 percent on a 30-year term, your payment would be $1,439. Over 30 years, you will pay $234,035.06 in interest alone!

If you double the payment to equal $2,878 per month for 10 years, you will pay $71,322.44 in interest and be mortgage free in a one-third of the time! This is saving you over $162,000!

If you had spent that extra $1,439 a month on auto loans, credit cards and other debts, you would still be paying thousands but not building value or equity in your home. Think about that difference! You are saving $162,000 and earning hundreds of thousands in equity!

On one hand, a double mortgage payment seems so ridiculous and unachievable at first. But when you do the math and really examine the numbers, it is achievable, smart and saves you tons of money. It helps you become a real homeowner and live with far less debt after!

Now one thing that we haven't mentioned about the 7–10 plan is that it assumes you are starting this plan from day one. If you are already 5 years into paying a 30-year loan, it will be a little faster and still save over $75,000 in interest! No matter where you are (nearly done, halfway done or just a few years in) paying a double payment will make a major impact on your mortgage.

This is also a good time to consider refinancing. When we began the 7–10 mortgage plan, it was with our original 30-year mortgage at 4.25 percent. At that point we could easily make a double mortgage payment. But we also wanted to find out what it would require if we refinanced at a lower rate for 15 years to cut the interest savings dramatically and THEN made double mortgage payments. After investigating, we found a rate and loan that would cut our mortgage from a 30-year with 24 years left to a 15-year loan. With the change in the interest rate and the balance carried over, our new refinanced payment was only $124 a month more. With the new 15-year loan, we could still easily make a double mortgage payment. So, investigating a refinancing option for fewer years at a lower interest rate could be a good way to get the ball rolling in your situation, even if you can't quite make double payments. Merely dropping from a 30-year to a 15-year mortage saves you quite a bit in interest while usually only minimally raising the monthly payment. Then when you can, make double payments or at least apply extra when you can and cut that down to a 10-year payoff, saving a lot in the process.

If you can't, there are a few extra little things you can do in the meantime while you work toward that 7–10 mortgage plan. Apply these tips when and where you can. By doing so, you can save an average of $50,000, but you might just hit that 7–10 year goal with just these steps.

Step 1–Implement a biweekly payment system.
Call your mortgage lender and set up a biweekly payment.

What is a biweekly payment? In a nutshell, it is dividing your monthly mortgage payment in half and paying that amount every two weeks.

The first important thing to understand is that this is different than *paying twice per month*. Paying twice per month will not really save you any money on your mortgage, but paying *every two weeks instead* is where savings are found.

Why is this the case? Your mortgage is calculated at 12, once-a-month payments. But since there are odd days in each month, a total year is not 12 × 4 = 48 weeks, but rather 52 weeks. So by paying every two weeks, you actually end up making an extra payment each year due to those extra four weeks. This extra payment will count 100 percent towards your principal balance if set up correctly.

Again, this is different than a half payment twice a month. A half payment twice per month is still paying the same 12 payments. Making this one extra payment per year at minimum will save the average homeowner about $30,000 to $60,000 in interest!

Let's illustrate using our same average home price of $284,000 and average interest rate of 4.5 percent over 30 years, but we will calculate with only the biweekly payments, amounting to one extra payment per year.

Mortgage Comparison			
Monthly Payment	$1,438.99	**Biweekly Payment**	$719.49
Total Interest	$234,035.06	**Total Interest**	$192,798.61
Avg Interest Each Month	$650.10	**Avg Interest Each Biweekly Period**	$246.55

This simple plan already saves over $41,000 for this average homeowner. The loan is also paid off 5½ years earlier.

We also suggest switching to a biweekly payment as soon as you are debt free as it actually makes budgeting and planning easier. For many households, it's much easier to make a $719.49 house payment each paycheck than a $1,438.99 payment every other paycheck. At this point, neither payment should be an issue; however, it is nice to have the mortgage more evenly divided for overall budgeting ease and planning. So it ends up really being a nice, practical way to pay your bills, and get that interest savings benefit.

We started doing this shortly after declaring, "We're debt free" and continued to do this until our other accounts and goals were funded, and until we were at the stage to be able to implement the 7–10 plan.

Step 2–Round up your biweekly payments to the nearest $100 amount.

Using our example of a $284,000 home, previously, we determined that a biweekly payment would result in a $719.49 payment. If you round this up to $800, this is an extra $161 a month. How does this affect the overall results?

By adding this extra step, you will now pay $158,491.52 in interest, saving $75,543.54 and paying the loan off 6½ years earlier than the original loan term!

Step 3–Pay as much extra as you can, when you can.

We hope that the message we are sending in this chapter is that anything extra you can put towards your mortgage is going to save you loads of money, shave off a fair amount of time and result in the amazing benefit of putting you closer and closer to being a homeowner.

This step only propels the plan further. Pay as much extra as you can, when you can.

A Word Of Encouragement

We want to end this chapter with the encouragement for those of you that are currently renting or saving up for your first house. With a bit of passion, strategy and sacrifice for a short time, you could own a home free and clear in 7 to 10 years. How amazing would it be to be a homeowner from day one? It never hurts to make buying a house with cash a goal. Worst case, you could put down a significant down payment on your house and become a real homeowner just a few short years later. What a great place to be financially!

Chapter 19

It's What We Weren't Talking About

By: Cassie

As we have shared this whole plan with you, there can oftentimes be a need to really drive a few points home. One of those is communication.

Towards the end of those initial three years of our debt payoff we began naturally starting to notice a difference in our attitude towards our debt and towards each other. Certain behaviors or attitudes developed in those early years that would become foundational for our success later. Not because some expert shared with us the magical nugget of truth, but more because they evolved and developed slowly through our failed attempts.

In many ways these concepts developed naturally even without us realizing it. We didn't open our eyes one day and look at each other and decide upon the contents of this chapter, rather many of the concepts presented here developed organically and then one day we opened our eyes to realize that these were the keys to our success.

Had our communication been lacking, we might not have seen the success that we shared in this book previously. That's why we feel the need to address this and a couple more critical factors that may be the extra ticket you need in your situation to help you see your financial goals through.

Communication

Perhaps you are reading this book and appreciating the ideas and hope for your debts and finances but realize the only path towards true success will be found by getting others in your family on board. This chapter is written to help you do just that.

Four additional steps to keep communication going throughout this process

Once you and your spouse have had your initial meeting and filled out the questionnaire (see page 51), there are some communication ground rules to keep the lines of communication continuously open, honest and real for continued and ensured success.

- Nightly meeting—Yes, we encourage you and your spouse to have a nightly meeting. This is also a good opportunity for your kids to be involved. No, we are not talking about a lengthy, parliamentary procedure kind of meeting, and unless your spouse is named Robert, there's no need to invite him. This is just a quick five minute or less meeting about the day's progress, successes and failures. It can be held even over the dinner table. A nightly check-in is a wonderful way to keep the communication open, stay on track, encourage one another and help you achieve those small milestones. Accountability and teamwork are going to be essential to this process, and this nightly meeting accomplishes both of these while paving the way for open communication. During the meeting, each family member should share what they spent that day, any expenses expected for the next day and any unexpected expenses coming up. This meeting helps increase accountability and helps identify issues before they become too large. These short daily meetings have one purpose—fostering open, easy communication between all family members in the household. Don't miss the points addressed in this chapter and encouragements to make this an integral part of implementing the 2% Rule in your family's life. You just might find your family ready to jump on board and commit to further months after seeing how painless and easy it is in the initial months.
- Setting a spending threshold—This is basically an allowance. Yes, you need an allowance, but you really need a concrete spending limit! Unlike a child that is handed the cash and not generally able to access the bank account to obtain more, you have that ability. If you have a spending threshold, it keeps your spending in check. This can be set for any amount that you choose. This is also so much more than an allowance. This particular rule really is another level of accountability. If you set a certain amount of money, that means you can spend that money without talking to your spouse. It's free for you to spend how you want. But if something costs more than that, you need to call or talk in person with your spouse about this purchase. Ultimately, it greatly reduces frivolous spending.

When we first started this process, our spending threshold was $5. If I wanted to buy something over $5, I needed to talk to Alex. It really made me think twice before I bought yet another pair of shoes, even if they were $10. I had to call and say, "Hey babe, can I buy another pair of shoes? They are only $10?" Alex would say something like, "But how many do you have now? Do you really need them?" and talk me through it. Often I would just walk away from the potential purchase because I didn't want to call him over that. This is the same process Alex goes through with me when he is tempted to spend more than we agreed upon. Once we were debt free, we raised the threshold to be $20. As the years have gone by and we have become more financially secure and free, we've increased this threshold and we revisit the subject often to keep our personal spending in check.

- Balancing the budget is for both of you—Granted, one spouse might actually do the bill paying, balancing and organizing, but both spouses should be involved. For many years, we actually both sat down together to pay our bills biweekly on payday. This was in addition to the nightly meeting. When it was time to actually pay things, we both wrote checks, we both saw the numbers being balanced and we both came up to speed on the accounts. Again, this doesn't mean that one spouse cannot primarily be acting as the bill payer and balancer, but both of you should know what is going on and neither should be in the dark!

- Finally, spouses need to have a joint bank account—If you are married, we do believe that it is crucial for your financial future and success to have a joint bank account. Operating separate bank accounts makes room for more frivolous spending, separate ideas of money, issues of honesty and trust, and puts a barrier between the two of you. Money is a very sensitive subject in a marriage. It is one of the most fought about topics. Ironically, we rarely fought about money because we didn't talk about it. However, according to a nationwide survey, money is the number one topic for arguments in 70 percent of households, with 21 percent of those money fights regarding hiding purchases from one another. Not only do Steps 1, 2 and 3 above address this, but Step 4 seals the deal. If you both have a bank account together, it protects each of you, keeps you honest and keeps the money topic real. Let's also not forget that when you marry someone, you are agreeing to become one, agreeing to live as one. You can't live as one when one of the most intimate topics in a relationship is money and you try to separate it. It needs to be managed together. Remember, it's "our money," not his, not hers.

Communicating with children

Teach your children that you live on a budget and decide ahead of time where the money is going.

- Set these ground rules beforehand and teach them these rules at home. Have a family meeting to discuss these ground rules and regularly remind and review these rules.
- Teach them about budgeting by allowing them to help in the process of saving money and helping to find ways to stretch the budget. My kids like to clip coupons, collect the digital coupons on the savings apps and do other easy tasks to help reach the budget goals.
- Let them participate in the family money meeting often so that they can learn about their family's finances and begin to develop a strong financial grounding.

For your older children, a positive step can include being honest with mistakes you've made with the finances. At that point, admitting that just because you have failed or haven't been very diligent does not mean you can continue to be neglectful. Changes will be made, and sacrifices will need to be made by all. The conversation is probably going to need to be much more extensive in regards to examples of how you have allowed the finances to slip away and what you should have done differently and how you plan to do things differently starting now. The specifics of the conversation are going to be different for each family, but at the basic start—that admission and apology from you is going to make all of the difference!

Good news for you and your teenager

Communicating a change in lifestyle to your teen may be more difficult than with younger children. However, once you have admitted that you made mistakes and mishandled money, there may be some positive outcomes.

- Your teen sees you as a humble, gracious adult that is mature enough to live up to your own mistakes.
- You have just gained a fair amount of respect over what you may have already gained over the years.
- Your teen will view you as treating them as an equal and that you respect them as a person and as a valuable part of your household, bettering your relationship with your teen.

Tell your teen about how this is going to be a gradual change that will yield big results if the whole family is committed, but it's not an overnight lifestyle change, so it will be easier. They will love this plan compared to the crash-diet approach!

You are giving your teen a great monetary foundation that they will hopefully take with them as they leave home and make much better decisions from the beginning, especially if you involve them in the process.

Other practical ways to get your teen and older child involved

- Your teen can also fill out the questionnaire on page 51 or less formally, you could discuss your teen's future and how that can fit into your family's financial goals.
- Involve your teen in setting the family's goals and the family's vision. They need to own this too to have a little more invested in these goals.
- Ask your teen to help find ways to cut the budget each month and to actively participate in making that happen!
- Involve your teen with finding ways to increase the family's income, paying them a portion of it as well.
- Start a savings account for your teen, teaching them how to disburse their funds. We generally follow the rule: Give 10 percent, Save 50 percent and Spend 40 percent. This is the best time to develop a love of giving, from the start. The longer you delay in giving, the harder it is for a person to give. However, if your child has lofty educational goals, we would suggest a life of saving before even starting a spending habit while still allowing for some sort of spending allowance so they are not frustrated. Anything outside of the planned budget they would like can be discussed and potentially worked into the budget if other sacrifices are made, with their help, or they can also work for those desires on their own.
- Have your teen immediately inform you of any financial needs like sports uniforms or school trips so that they can help in finding ways to work it in while working towards the family's goals.
- Be a living example. Your teen needs to witness you putting into practice what you preach. If you didn't follow the plan you need to confess and repent to the whole family. Demonstrate joy, happiness and freedom in meeting financial goals and becoming increasingly more financially free! Celebrate those small milestones.
- Start talking to your teen about the idea of being a real homeowner earlier in life than most anyone else with the 7–10 plan and get them excited about their future.

When it comes to your extended family, although spending time out could be a partial issue, most of the money concerns here are the gift expectations during the holidays, family gatherings or reunions or family vacations. If you are honest with your family, if they really love and respect you, they will respect you wanting to be better off financially. If they are willing to make sacrifices instead of choosing a family trip to the Bahamas, perhaps they could choose a family camping trip a few hours away. There are so many alternatives and ways to encorage your extended family to adjust to not create a financial burden for you and your immediate family.

As far as gifts go, when we first started our journey, we talked to our parents and our siblings about how the gifts would probably be different in the near future. We told them that we were working to get out of debt, and we needed to make budget cuts, including in the gift department. In exchange, we gave them the expectations from us and asked them to not "go all out" or keep the gifts simple. We didn't think it would be fair to say, "We are cutting back on gifts for you, but still expect the same level of gifts from you." That's just silly! Ask that they don't spend or spend very little on you. We did this and our families were completely understanding and in fact, grateful that we respected them enough to set those expectations. Regardless, our parents have still gone above and beyond because they want to, but have never placed that obligation, guilt or feeling upon us!

Communication with our friends and family opened up a whole new level of success for us. We didn't tell them the story you are reading. It wasn't necessary. All we needed to say was simply, "We have some big financial goals we are trying to hit, including getting out of debt."

Of course, now that that life is behind us, we are telling the world the details of our story in hopes that it will change your life too! But in the midst of it, it was too difficult and embarrassing for us to reveal.

Communication is key—and if it doesn't exist, you'll find it nearly impossible to succeed in meeting your goals. Make this happen and be intentional about doing so.

That leads us into our final thoughts—what does it mean to be intentional?

Chapter 20

Two More Critical Factors

By: Alex

There are two other factors we developed in the process of our own journey that we want to share in this chapter, the ideas of intentional living and giving. Let's review each and see how they fit into the turning points we found as critical steps towards establishing our debt payoff plan.

Be Intentional

What is the concept of intentional living? On our website, we encourage these exact concepts as part of our 30-Day Be Intentional Challenge. This challenge helps the participants work towards understanding the importance of living intentionally in every area of life. Once you understand that a key component behind success in life is living intentionally, your future opens up and life becomes yours to live.

First, let's define living intentionally. Intentional living is organizing your life, your home, your finances and your schedule in such a way that the result is a well-ordered life. In many ways it's a result of applying a common-sense type approach to living life.

Remember the sample day in a life not lived intentionally on page 9? When you live without intent, things just seem to happen in a cascading cycle of less than ideal events.

One of the first things we encourage families to do when they are getting started in the process of wanting to seriously pay off their debts is to participate in our 30-Day Be Intentional Challenge. We refer to each day's challenge as baby steps, or steps so small that they seem insignificant by themselves; however, once you string them together they form a whole system that transforms your life.

Sure, some of them might sound a bit silly. One of the day's baby steps is to make your bed that morning. We found that taking an extra two or three minutes in the morning helps get your mind that much more organized for the day and started off on the right foot.

Another day, our challenge is to Do Dinner by 10. For those that stay at home, this means having your plan for dinner that day figured out by 10 a.m. This includes knowing what you plan to make, having the ingredients ready and even throwing it into a slow cooker if applicable. For those that work outside the home, this refers to 10 p.m. the night before. You can easily see that taking those *moments* will keep you from having to either buy dinner out for your family and give you the chance to make a healthier option because you now have the time to mentally and physically prepare what you need for the meal.

In other words, making intentional decisions gives you the ability to exert more control in your life. Sure, we understand that life comes at you fast and that emergencies arise or other circumstances can fly in your face and keep you from having the organized day you want. The plan, however, is to minimize those days and make the norm for your family an organized expectation.

What's great about this as well is that you start taking control of your time. Now, instead of finding yourself at the end of the day with little to show for it, you are able to control the events of the day and you find yourself with more time than you thought you had before.

Our encouragement to you is to communicate with your spouse and your family and find ways to become more intentional in your lives. Obviously we would encourage you to consider our 30-Day Be Intentional Challenge, but however you decide to go about it, the important thing is that you do something.

Yes, you heard that right: we're encouraging you to be intentional about finding ways to *be intentional* in your life.

Once you do that, that fictitious story in Chapter 1 can be exactly that, and your new future can be an organized reality.

At that point, you might see taking the steps to be intentional with your finances is a natural next step. You are now at a point where you can start telling your money where to go and actually decide whether you want to go out for a quick lunch with your co-workers because you want to as an occasional treat, instead of because you *have to,* day in and day out.

Giving

There was yet another critical point in our 180-degree turnaround, and that was a different mindset and attitude towards giving. Yes, we are talking about giving and charity even when we were so far in debt. Learning to have freedom and happiness in giving created a whole new attitude, contributing to a change in our mindset.

You see, previously, we thought we were in too much trouble to give. We thought we were so far in debt that the most important thing to do was to get out of debt as fast as possible and then make up our giving after we were debt free.

Let's be honest, this rarely happens for anyone. We were hoarding all of our money and all of our assets for ourselves, and justifying it by saying we needed to get out of debt, that *this was the most important step* we could take at that time of our lives.

No, it wasn't. It only further sealed in our minds a love of money and a desire for money in an unhealthy way. We were not poor or needy. Yes, we had nothing left over after each paycheck. Yes, we were deep in debt. But when we realized that we were hoarding every last penny for our own success and our own goals, we realized how selfish, unhappy and rude we were. How heartless in some sense.

One example of our selfishness during this time was displayed by our lack of giving to our local church. We justified it by saying, "We can't give right now; we will make up for this after we are out of debt."

A major turning point in our lives came when we realized our selfishness was so deep-seated that we had indeed become uncharitable and unloving to the world around us. Because we had started communicating openly to each other about our money and finances, it quickly became clear to both of us how much our lack of giving was affecting us. We both felt disappointed and guilty about being so selfish. Thankfully, once we honestly and openly began communicating, we both realized how our selfishness was far beyond affecting the two of us, but how it was also impacting the world around us. This small example is yet another demonstration regarding the importance of open communication about money.

For us, our opportunities for giving came in multiple fashions. First, we decided that part of our budget HAD to include giving and charity. For our family, we decided that a minimum of 10 percent of our income was a good starting point. With our change of heart and attitude, we wanted to give. It became a deep desire for us to give, not a burden or a stress at all!

In fact, this became so important to us during this turning point, that whenever a paycheck came in, the amount we were to give was the first thing calculated in the budget. Not only did we give the minimum of 10 percent, we gave extra when we could.

Second, not only did we allocate money directly for giving, but we also gave our time to church and community charities around us. This was a free giving option and yet, *we hadn't been doing this either* up to that point. Again, our prior attitude focused on us and our narrow-minded goal: get out of debt as fast as possible, throwing every penny and ounce of our time to it.

Third, we also freely gave of our physical resources like food from our food pantry, clothing and homeless care kits we made. This wasn't necessarily a free option, although much of it was, but even the physical items were purchased very affordably. Because of our frugal lifestyle, we were able to stretch our own dollars to give more value than the charity would obtain just from the value of the money donated.

Let us share with you the financial impact that giving of at least 10 percent of our income, our physical resources, food and time did for us with our *tight* budget and our plan to get out of this debt.

Well, amazing things!

In fact, we didn't even notice the 10 percent leaving the door from the top. It didn't affect us at all. All we saw was sheer success in a new, big way, like we had never experienced before. We had more than enough to meet our 2 percent goals each month and ultimately succeed in a very big way just a few short years later, all with giving consistently as the top priority every time new money came in.

Now we are not saying that this is some sort of magical experience that once you start giving that money will magically flow in and you will get more than 10 percent extra back. Not at all. But we believe that our change in attitude in becoming cheerful givers helped change our own attitudes about money.

As you have been reading our story, you know that we failed and failed miserably those first few years of our attempted debt payoff journey. We would be on track, throwing all the money we could to our debt, even down to every last penny, and then we would *break* and splurge on ourselves with the result of two steps forward and one step back.

However, for us, this change in attitude and in heart of putting others first through giving changed our lives.

Nothing is different today except that we try to give more and more, serve others and serve our community in more ways. We still know that a heart that joyfully gives has a more full life than any amount of debt freedom or any amount of monetary success can bring.

Even when we started our website at TheThriftyCouple.com, we picked a charity and decided, from the beginning, that a portion of our proceeds would be donated to that charity.

Lastly, we hope you can see that we were able to adopt from other concepts discussed to this point: Open communication helped us identify our lack of giving problem and discuss how to move forward. Intentional living helped us to find creative and unique ways to give and to give even more than we originally thought possible. Applying these concepts to everything you do in this financial journey will help you towards further financial success.

We hope to become increasingly more and more charitable and giving in the days and years ahead.

Chapter 21

Your Journey Begins

By: Both

We have given you so much information and so many details on how to implement our plan in this book. As we end our book your journey is about to begin. We want to remind you of the steps and encourage you so that no matter where you are in your journey, you can find the step you're on and move forward from there.

Don't forget these two simple rules as you move through each step of the process:

- Rule 1—Stay Out of Debt
- Rule 2—Stick with the 2% Rule for Life

Lastly, we want to share a summary of the steps one final time so you can see them in one concise whole. Review them and go back to find the details of each step.

- Step 1—Build Emergency Fund Quickly (page 136)
- Step 2—Pay Off All Consumer Debt Using 2% Rule (page 138)
- Step 3—Set Up Biweekly Mortgage Payments (page 139)
- Step 4—Contribute the Maximum On Your 401(k) for Company Match (page 139)
- Step 5—Build 3 to 6 Months Of Savings (page 139)
- Step 6—Contribute The Remaining Retirement 15% Into a Roth IRA (page 140)
- Step 7—Set Up Your Cash and Percentage-Based Savings and Add Your Contributions (page 140)

- Step 8—Contribute the Maximum Household Allowance for a Roth IRA (page 140)

- Step 9—Round Mortgage Payments to the Nearest $100 (page 141)

- Step 10—Fund Businesses (page 141)

- Step 11—Pay Extra Towards Mortgage (page 141)

- Step 12—Implement the 7–10 Mortgage Plan (page 142)

- Step 13—Decide Your Next Financial Investments snd Steps (page 142)

We Are Real And We Are Here

Have you ever read a book and craved more the second you closed it? Have you ever read a book and wanted to meet with, talk to and share with the author of the book about the discoveries you made, your ideas, your plans and your goals? We have. But yet, when we turn the pages and come closer to the ending, there is no opportunity to talk with the author but rather only a last page.

But that is not where we want our book to end. We want our book to end as you close these pages and the cover to stand up, take a deep breath and meet us online at TheThriftyCouple.com! We are real and we are reachable!

You can talk to us, you can share your successes with us, and yes, even your failures along the way. We've been there, we've taken this journey and we are still on a journey. You can receive encouragement and you can join with us along this journey. When you close this book, your journey is just beginning, not ending.

With that, our friends, we look forward to what your future holds. We look forward to you implementing the unique and the common strategies shared in this book to make for one successful, effective, sustainable approach to your debt and your finances.

Your future is bright!

You have options!

You have a plan!

You have hope!

When you close this book, your world opens up and it's time to get out there and makes things happen!

BACK TO WHERE IT ALL BEGAN

BY: ALEX

The door shut quietly behind me as I shuffled down to the foyer to check out of the hotel. As I walked, something was nagging at me and tugging on my emotions. I couldn't place it, and my mind searched to find its source.

Initially I was confused. Was I saddened that our anniversary trip had just come to an end and that in a few short hours we would be back at home preparing to get back to work the next day? Maybe it was the fog that still hovered over the beach and ocean as the sun waited for the right moment to burst through and make it all disappear.

It didn't take me long to realize that none of these were to blame. My mind zeroed in with razor-like focus on what was overwhelming my soul and my heart with grief. I could sum it all up in one word.

Fear.

It had been just sixteen years earlier that I had walked down the same hall to the same hotel lobby that started it all. Years before during that stroll, visions and dreams of what the rest of our honeymoon would bring filled my mind, only to be shattered just minutes later when the clerk would hand my credit card back to me, sharing that epic, life-changing news that my card had been declined.

Now I knew better. I reminisced over those memories permanently etched into my mind, as they would set the stage for those initial years of our marriage. Who am I kidding? Our lives have been forever scarred and yet transformed from the events that occurred during those formative days.

Even our financial state years from now in retirement is impacted, given that money we could have set aside while younger was instead spent foolishly on events, food and things long since forgotten.

With each step closer my fear grew. I knew the fear was irrational as Cassie and I had set aside the money for this trip, often joking that this trip would be far different than our first. We had planned our flights and hotel as frugally as we could to free up our trip budget for meals and souvenirs we had planned to purchase. As part of that we had even spoken to the hotel manager months before making the reservation, and we were thrilled that they offered us a sweet deal knowing it was our first time back since our honeymoon so many years before.

Just that morning I had even connected online to my bank, ironically the same bank that offered us that loan we talked about in the early pages of this book, to balance our budget with little to update on my spreadsheet since we had spent cash for the trip to that point. The balance I had seen would be more than enough to cover a lavish trip, although we had intentionally decided to enjoy our anniversary trip spending much less, choosing to reflect on each other while deciding to spend that money on other priorities.

That fear indeed was irrational, but present nonetheless. I couldn't shake it, so I simply chalked it up to an old wound in which the nerves could still occasionally feel the original pain.

I finally reached the front desk. To this day I'm still not sure why, but her words startled me.

"How was your stay, Mr. Michael?"

With all my thoughts chasing through my head I might have sounded trite. My nondescript reply probably came out mumbled at first. Not wanting to appear rude, I refocused and shared with her how much we enjoyed our stay and how special it was to be back years after our honeymoon at the exact same hotel.

As you might guess, I didn't share the details with her about how back then I couldn't initially pay the bill for our stay. That seemed a bit too raw for that encounter.

She next asked if I wanted to keep the full amount on my card. This time it was my debit card.

I knew what would happen as soon as I answered. Although the method might be different, I knew what was to come upon my simple acknowledgement. Less than a second after she clicked the button the same basic process would occur that happened years ago. Our account information would be transferred to a credit card processor that would inquire of my bank for our balance. Moments later the system she was working with would receive a response notifying her computer system with a code. This time, the hope was that it would be for an approval and not a declined transaction.

I nodded and held my breath, probably not much different than I did when I waited for the answer from that loan officer those many years ago. My stomach tightened and my head throbbed. Yes, all in less than a second.

"You're all set, Mr. Michael," came her reply.

I countered with a quick response and made my way back to our room. This time, instead of opening the door to our room to look at my beautiful bride with shame, I had a different response.

I still remember opening that door, glancing at my still beautiful bride of 16 years, smiling at her and simply saying the one thing I wish I could have said years before, "We're all good dear. Let's finish packing and make our way."

APPENDIX A: PRICE POINT CHART FOR GROCERIES

Normal Shopping And Price Comparison List

Tip: Write down the items you normally buy and keep track of the prices at the three stores you shop at most. This list is your reference so when you need to purchase that item you can check this list for the lowest everyday price. Plus if the item goes on sale, you can use this list to determine your price point and whether that sale is better than another store's price.

Store Price Comparison			
Item	Store #1	Store #2	Store #3
_____	_____	_____	_____
_____	_____	_____	_____
_____	_____	_____	_____
_____	_____	_____	_____
_____	_____	_____	_____
_____	_____	_____	_____
_____	_____	_____	_____
_____	_____	_____	_____
_____	_____	_____	_____
_____	_____	_____	_____
_____	_____	_____	_____

Appendix B: Annual Financial Summary

Developing Our Family Economy

We encourage you to sit down with your family annually to complete the following checklist. The goal of this is to help you start thinking outside of your daily, busy schedule and force you to work together on becoming intentional with your finances. We all know the adage: If you fail to plan, you plan to fail. And although it seems trite, we have found in our own experience just how true it is.

One of the most important lessons we learned in our own household is the idea of ensuring open communication and committing as a whole family to pursue this plan.

We recommend setting aside some time one evening as a family to enjoy together and as part of that take the time to work through this checklist. If that is too daunting, possibly try to work through it during a family meal. No matter how big or small, just try to do something. This is your checklist—do with it what you will! As one idea, prior to starting ask each family member the following questions:

- Is everyone in the family willing to participate?
- Are we ready to do an even better job this year (compared to previous years) with our budget?

Finally, keep this checklist as we want you to refer to it the full year. The making of the goals and decisions is the easy part – following through takes hard work, dedication and accountability. Are you ready to get started?

Overall Goals

What overall goals do we have for our family?
This can include non-financial goals as well, as every decision truly has a financial impact on the family. Unless the goals are identified and prepared for in advance, those last-minute preparations could be costly. Alternatively, if you don't financially plan for those large dreams of the family, they may never come to fruition.

Long term (3+ years):

Mid term (1–3 years):

Short term (this year):

Specific Goals For This Year

What savings goals do we want to achieve?

Are we trying to pay off debt? How much? Do we have a plan of attack?

What charities do we wish to support this year:

Do we want to plan on a vacation(s) this year? How much should we budget?
The goal here isn't to plan the details, but to keep the questions at a high level (the 30,000-foot view). Do you want to drive or fly? Is this a 2-week vacation or a couple of weekend camping trips?

(continued)

Specific Goals For This Year (continued)

How much should we budget for Christmas?
Start thinking now about what we would like to set aside for Christmas. Can we develop a plan to set aside a certain amount per month to get to our goal?

What events are coming up this year?
Birthdays, anniversary, celebration?

Do we need to prepare for a major purchase this year?

Plan Of Action

What are some initial actions we need to implement to meet the identified goals?
In the following weeks we will be identifying a more detailed approach – allow this meeting time to be a brainstorming session. Can you eliminate one or more meal out each month? Spend less on entertainment? Other ideas?

Do we want to work extra as a family to help with our goals?
What are the talents of each family member? Is someone good with marketing? With numbers?

What expectations do we have of each family member?

What is one thing each family member is willing to sacrifice to meet our goals?

Can we as a family commit to reaching the goals we've decided upon?

How are we going to keep each other accountable?

Appendix C: Recipes

Bulk Muffin Mix

This is a super easy, practical and affordable way to replace those boxed and pouch muffin mixes that you get in the store. Check the next page for more flavor and add-in options.

Yield: 6 batches of 12 muffins

8 cups (960 g) all-purpose flour or wheat flour

3 cups (300 g) of sugar

3 tbsp (40 g) baking powder

2 tsp (11 g) salt

2 tsp (4 g) cinnamon

2 tsp (4 g) nutmeg

Mix all of these dry items together and store in a container in your pantry for you to use when you need it!

Muffins

From the previous bulk muffin mix, use this recipe to bake scrumptious muffins for your family in a variety of flavors.

Yield: 12 muffins

2¾ cups (330 g) Bulk Muffin Mix (page 179)

1 beaten egg

1 cup (240 ml) of milk

½ cup (120 ml) melted butter

Preheat oven to 400°F (204°C). Mix the beaten egg, milk and butter together and pour into muffin mix. Mix with a fork until well blended. Add any add-ins and mix again.

Pour into a 12 cup muffin tin (⅔ full) or cake pan (for a cake like muffin) and bake at 400°F (204°C) for 18 to 22 minutes or until a toothpick comes out clean.

These taste good on their own, but here are some mix-in ideas that you can add at the time of preparation.

I usually add around a cup of something. Whether it will be half of this and a half of that for 1 cup total. As one example, I've added ¾ cup (90 g) of Craisins and ¼ cup (60 g) of brown sugar. My kids LOVED it!

Good add-ins: (add your ideas too!)

- Blueberries or other berries
- Apples
- Peaches
- Apricots
- Pumpkin puree
- Cranberries
- Craisins
- Raisins

- Cinnamon
- Brown sugar
- Chocolate chips
- Nuts
- Coconut
- Instant coffee granules
- Flax seeds
- Wheat germ

OR make them as they are and then once baked roll in melted butter then in a sugar–cinnamon mix for what are called "French Muffins" (one of my mom's traditional muffins for special occasion breakfasts!).

Taco/Mexican Seasoning Mix

Here's an easy recipe that is very versatile to use in many/all different types of Mexican themed foods like tacos, enchiladas, taco/tortilla soup, fajitas, chili, Mexican pasta—anything!

Yield: Equivalent to 8 envelopes of taco seasoning

6 tbsp (48 g) chili powder

2 tsp (5 g) garlic powder

2 tsp (5 g) onion powder

2 tsp (3 g) red pepper flakes (or to taste)

2 tsp (3 g) oregano

1½ tsp (3 g) paprika

3 tbsp (20 g) ground cumin

2 tsp (11 g) salt

1½ tsp (3 g) pepper

In a small bowl, mix all of the ingredients together. Store in an airtight container. The mix will store for a long time.

To use: 2 tablespoons (12 g) is equal to one envelope of store-bought seasoning. Adjust recipes accordingly.

This recipe will make around 8 batches of recipes requiring 1 envelope of seasoning.

Soup or Sauce (SOS) Mix

This frugal make-ahead and store recipe can be used as a replacement for creamed soups in any recipe, as well as the base for other sauces, gravies, soups and much more! It is also fat free.

Yield: Equivalent to nine 10¾ ounce (318 ml) cans of creamed soups

2 cups (250 g) powdered non-fat dry milk

¾ cup (83 g) cornstarch

¼ cup (24 g) instant chicken bouillon

2 tbsp (10 g) dried onion flakes

2 tsp (3 g) of Italian seasoning or a combination of dried parsley, oregano and basil

1 tsp black pepper

Make the mix by combining all of the dry ingredients until blended.

Store in a resealable bag or container to use when needed. It can be stored on the shelf! No need to refrigerate.

Instructions to substitute for one 10¾ ounce (318 ml) can of creamed soup: Combine ⅓ cup (80 g) of dry mix with 1¼ cups (300 ml) of cold water. Cook and stir on the stove top or in the microwave until thickened.

Add thickened mixture to the casseroles/recipes just as you would a can of soup.

Homemade Laundry Soap

Save "loads" of money by making your very own detergent that is very easy (I can make mine in less than 10 minutes) and have it be very effective in gently cleaning your clothing!

Yield: 40 to 80 loads worth of detergent

5 oz (142 g) bar Fels Naptha soap

2 cups (480 ml) super washing soda

2 cups (480 ml) borax

5–6 drops lavender essential oil (or other fragrance if you prefer)

Microwave the Fels Naptha soap bar for 30 to 60 seconds to soften the bar.

Cut it into cubes and put it in a blender/food processor. Add half of the borax and washing soda and blend. Add the remaining borax and washing soda and blend until uniform.

Drop 5 to 6 drops of essential oil into the mixture and then blend for 20 to 30 seconds so that the fragrance is evenly distributed.

Your final product will be a nice fluffy peach-colored powder detergent that smells great and works well! We store it in a plastic container in our laundry room. Use 1 tablespoon (15 g) a load and 2 tablespoons (30 g) for a heavy load.

Disclaimer: Before using any homemade laundry detergent, please be sure to test it on a small piece of clothing first.

Best Window Cleaner

This is the BEST homemade window and glass cleaner that doubles as a beautiful stainless steel cleaner too!

Yield: 1 spray bottle of cleaner

Any size spray bottle

Equal parts water to equal parts white distilled vinegar to fill bottle

4 drops lavender or lemon essential oil per 4 oz (120 ml) of liquid

1 drop of dish soap per 4 oz (120 ml) of liquid

Funnel (optional)

Pour the equal parts of water and vinegar in your bottle and add the dish soap.

Add your drops of essential oil. Put the sprayer back on and shake until blended.

Dishwasher Powdered Soap

This homemade dishwasher powdered soap works well as a cheap, natural and effective alternative to store-bought soap and ends up coasting about $0.05 per load.

Yield: Approximately 23 loads

1 cup (240 ml) borax

1 cup (240 ml) washing soda

1 packet of unsweetened powdered drink mix or 2 tbsp (30 ml) citric acid

¼ cup (60 ml) coarse salt

10 drops citrus essential oil

Add all of the dry ingredients and mix until well blended. Use a fork to mix as it breaks up the lumps.

Add the citrus oil and the mix thoroughly. Pour into a container.

Label and provide instructions on use. Your dishwasher could be different, but I add 1 tablespoon (15 ml) to the closed compartment and ½ tablespoon (7 ml) to the open compartment. You may need to adjust these measurements accordingly. This is about three-weeks worth of detergent for us.

All-Purpose Cleaner

Use this one cleaner to do the cleaning job of many.

Yield: 20 ounces

1 tbsp (15 g) borax

2 cups (475 ml) hot tap water

½ cup (120 ml) 3% hydrogen peroxide

4–6 drops dish soap

10 drops tea tree essential oil

7 drops oregano essential oil

10 drops lavender essential oil

20 oz spray bottle

Place the borax in a shallow bowl. Then pour the hot water on top and mix with a fork, spoon or whisk until dissolved.

Using a funnel for ease, pour this mixture into a bottle. Add the hydrogen peroxide and stir in the 4–6 drops of dish soap. Add all of your oils. Put the lid/spray nozzle on your bottle and shake to blend well.

To make a super cleaner, spray the surface with 3 percent acidic vinegar prior to spraying this solution. The combination of these two together make it a super-effective cleaner.

NOTE: Mixing the vinegar with this cleaner in the same bottle will lessen the effectiveness. The addition of the vinegar only works if sprayed separately.

Moisturizing Foaming Hand Soap

You can easily make your own moisturizing, foaming hand soap with a few simple ingredients.

Yield: 12 ounces (355 ml) of liquid hand soap

2–3 tbsp (30–45 ml) liquid castile soap

Foaming soap dispenser (buy one, use it and then refill moving forward)

½ tbsp (7 ml) vegetable glycerin

5–10 drops favorite essential oils

8–12 oz (240–360 ml) water

Add the liquid castile soap to the foaming dispenser. Add the vegetable glycerin and essential oils.

Carefully add enough water to fill nearly to the top (leaving enough room for the pump). Attach the pump and shake vigorously.

Facial Toner Recipe

It's easy to make your own facial toner and it only takes two ingredients.

Yield: 4 ounces of toner

4 oz (120 ml) witch hazel

5–10 drops essential oil for skin (like lavender)

Mix in a small bottle and keep sealed and away from direct sunlight. Use like you would any other toner.

RESOURCES

- thethriftycouple.com/2percentbookresources

About The Authors

Alex and Cassie began their lives together with the wedding that started their financial demise back in 1999. Since then, they journeyed deeply into debt together and dug themselves out using the concepts learned along the way, contained in the book you hold in your hands. All of this while falling deeper in love with each other throughout their struggles, pain and even those gradual successes that got them to the point where they are today.

They became known as The Thrifty Couple after starting their website by the encouragement of a friend. Each person they met was amazed at their financial journey and the innovative way they paid off their debts—to the point they were repeating their story and tips time and time again—almost daily. That friend thought documenting that process online with tips and encouragement to other readers would help thousands through their own journey, offering them hope and the tools they need to find their own success in their own finances.

To date, their website has reached tens of millions of households. They have since spread their message and 2% Rule through speaking engagements, podcast, radio and television interviews. The more people they can reach with their message of hope the better.

When not writing and speaking, Alex and Cassie love to be with their kids hiking in the Rocky Mountains, playing games, running races, learning new things and enjoying reading out loud as a family at night.

Cassie thrives on maximizing her life and searching for her next challenge whether for the blog or her children. If she's not working on that next idea she can be found snuggling with her kids and helping teach and encourage them to follow a better path financially and in all of life. She has truly found that her passion is in writing and this book has sealed the deal. She wants to consider writing additional books, whether on finances or fiction.

Alex has ninja skills as a database programmer by day and a debt-slashing financial advisor by night. In 2015, Alex used the principles of the 2% Rule to lose almost 100 pounds and has transformed his life and mindset into one of healthy living. He has kept the weight off since and is working towards nutrition and personal fitness certifications to begin his new chapter to help others in this area of their life as well! When he's not working or studying, he's finding time with his family or following his passion for running; whether on the road or on a trail he's chasing his next running goal.

ACKNOWLEDGMENTS

We thank our friends and family for their patience over these last 18 years of our lives. We have learned much from each of you and know that much of where we are at today is because of bits of advice you gave us throughout our journey. Though you might not have known how dark our financial lives were (we can only imagine your surprise as you read this book) we are grateful for so many that encouraged us even when you might not have known just how terribly we needed it.

We thank Jessica Williams for her encouragement to start our website with the purpose of sharing our story and encourage others on their own financial journey. We may have never become known as The Thrifty Couple, had it not been for you putting the bug into Cassie's ear so many years ago.

We can't share our appreciation enough to Catherine Ellis for her hours of review in the initial stages of this book. Her encouragement and excitement to get the next set of chapters from us helped motivate us to move forward. Neither of us claim to be professional writers and know that without your patience, love and pens of red ink we wouldn't be where we are at today.

We thank Marissa and Will at Page Street and the many others that helped us through this process as well. You took a chance on us when you heard a couple share their crazy story and passion for helping others.

We can't even share how much we love our children and have appreciated their patience through this process. Although we know the hours dedicated to writing this book would be short in the grand scheme of things, you were patient with us even when it seemed it would never end.

Finally, we cannot forget all of our amazing readers of TheThriftyCouple.com. Your interactions with us have been invaluable to help us continue towards putting the finishing touches on the process and ideas you see here. We can't thank those of you enough that have written us words of encouragement over these last years. We really did start our site with the intent of helping as many families as possible and are grateful from those of you that have shared that our intent was not in vain.

To those who are entering the finances realm
And are debating whether debt is the answer.
We invite you to learn from our mistakes.

To those who are so far in debt they can't
See the light at the end of the tunnel.
Trust us, we've been there and you can find it!

To those that have never trodden the path
We have followed and have wisely
Never known a penny of debt.
Stay that way.

To the rest
We encourage you to learn from our mistakes,
Learn from our gained experience and wisdom
And let's walk this path together.

In sum—we are grateful for you.

INDEX